All Access: Unlocking the Power of God's Word

Stacie L. Buck

All Access:
Unlocking the Power of God's Word

Stacie L. Buck

Diamond Shapers
INTERNATIONAL, LLC
Transforming Minds, Transforming Lives

All Access: Unlocking the Power of God's Word

Published by Diamond Shapers International, LLC
850 NW Federal Highway, Suite 427
Stuart, FL 34994
www.diamondshapers.com

Cover design by PhotoGraphics USA
www.photographicsusa.com

For bulk sales contact Diamond Shapers International, LLC
Email: info@diamondshapers.com
Phone: (772) 287-8849

ISBN-13: 978-0692208526

ISBN-10: 0692208526

Acknowledgements

...thanks be to God, Who gives us the victory [making us conquerors] through our Lord Jesus Christ.

~ I Corinthians 15:57 AMP

First and foremost, I want to thank God for His power and glory at work in my life and for leading me on the journey that brought me to write this book.

Mom, Dad and Bryan, thank you for your unconditional love and support in all my endeavors and for always believing in me and encouraging me.

Jenny Price, thank you for all of your coaching and encouragement as well as for the gift of accountability through Mastermind group.

Tammy Schaefer, thank you for allowing me to bounce ideas off of you and for providing feedback to me.

Kim Stingo, thank you for introducing me to such life changing revelation and for your many years of friendship.

Debra Campany, thank you for encouraging me and mentoring me. Your support means so very much to me.

Holly McPherson, thank you for inviting me to the Champions Workshop. Little did I know attending would be an invaluable part of my journey.

George Hope, I am forever thankful you entered my life at the exact moment you did bringing me much needed hope and happiness and for being a part of my journey. I will always treasure the special moments we had together.

Last but not least, thank you to the ladies who allowed me to be part of their transformation and for being such a captive audience: Danielle, Sue, Deborah, Merle, Ceceila, Eileen, Michele, & Kendra.

TABLE OF CONTENTS

Preface

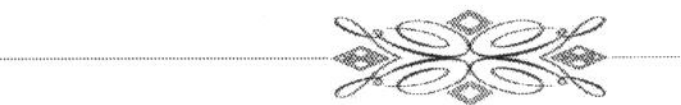

I can remember that time in my life quite vividly. It was January 2010 and I was filled with anticipation of what the year would bring. My healthcare consulting business had finally gained momentum and I had more work coming in than I could keep up with and I was making more money than ever before. I had finally broken through a plateau I had been on for several years. After facing some struggles at the end of 2008 and through 2009, I was certain 2010 would one of the best years of my entire life and the first several months of 2010 certainly didn't disappoint. I had no idea that on May 25, 2010 my life would begin to spiral out of control.

That day started off as any other day. One filled with the hustle and bustle of working on several projects. The past few months had been a particularly stressful time, many weeks working seven days a week to meet the obligations to my clients. I had no idea when I woke up that morning my day would be capped off with an emergency room visit that would be the first of many encounters with medical professionals. Over the next seven months I experienced two more trips to the emergency room and consultations with ten different doctors; none of which provided any solid answers to what was causing my debilitating illness. While I was stuck in my pit of hopelessness and despair, I had no idea this horrific event would be a turning point in my life.

By January of 2011 as my condition began to spontaneously improve, I started to do some soul searching. The purpose in all of this was to understand my own behaviors. Furthermore, I didn't understand why many of my relationships were shallow and dysfunctional and why I was unfulfilled in spite of having a list of accomplishments a mile long. I had wrongly convinced myself that I was perfectly fine and that those around me had serious problems.

In my search, I came across the book *Attachments: Why You Love, Feel and Act the Way You Do* by Dr. Tim Clinton. Little did I know reading this book would serve as the beginning of "Stacie 101" - course work carefully arranged by God Himself. Shortly after reading this book, I was introduced to teachings by *Elijah House Ministries* and the following year I came into contact with a wonderful couple working with *Restoring the Foundations Ministry*. In addition to encounters with these ministries, I also spent countless hours of personal study, reading numerous books and listening to many different teachings. I also attended two workshops hosted by Klemmer & Associates in the fall of 2012, the content of which reinforced what I had learned through ministry and it provided an even deeper level of revelation. Through these experiences I was able to uncover issues that were locked away deep inside my soul and causing havoc in my life. After almost three years of ministry and study, perfectly designed by God, I was no longer an angry frustrated person and I am pleased to say that I am now walking in freedom in areas that I never thought possible and I desire the same for you.

Please don't misunderstand me. I am not perfect. I am far from perfect. I am a work in progress. I am not yet where I want to be or need to be on my journey, but I thank God I am not where I used to be. For most of my adult life I was living frustrated, miserable and unfulfilled, yet to the outside world I seemed to have it all. I thought I was doing just fine all things considered. The interesting thing was I didn't realize how frustrated, angry and unhappy I really was until I wasn't anymore. To me, my inner turmoil seemed normal. Yours might seem to be to you as well.

We are living in a critical time in which operating in the full power of the Holy Spirit is a vital necessity. As Christians we are called to impact the world, but how can we have an impact on the world when our lives look much the same as unbelievers? We are called to be the light in a dark world, but unfortunately we are challenged to find our way out of our darkness. Although we are saved, we live in bondage because of issues deeply rooted in our soul and we are unable to fulfill God's will for our lives. If you feel as though you have been wandering around in the wilderness for most of your life, then I believe this book is for you. You can be the light in a dark world. You can have the life you desire. You can fulfill the will of God for your life. You can walk in victory.

This book was birthed out of my own journey of personal discovery and transformation. It is a compilation of knowledge from numerous sources as well as my own personal study. It is what I like to refer to as the "best of the best". Several years and thousands of dollars were spent on acquiring the knowledge and revelation in this book. It is my desire to make it available to all those who might otherwise be unable to spend a significant amount of time or money unlocking these mysteries. It is my hope and prayer by sharing principles learned during my personal journey of discovery and healing, I can help you identify hindrances holding you back from experiencing God's best for your life. It is my heart's desire to see the lives of others transformed by sharing much of the knowledge that has brought freedom into my own life in so many ways. If you are serious about changing your life and embracing God's best for you I believe this book will be a turning point for you.

Stacie L. Buck
President & Founder
Diamond Shapers International, LLC

Introduction

[10] The thief comes only in order to steal and kill and destroy. I came that they may have and enjoy life, and have it in abundance (to the full, till it [a]overflows).
~ John 10:10 AMP

A deeper study of John 10:10 reveals that our lives in Christ are to be superabundant in quantity and superior in quality.[1] This kind of life is promised to us not only after we leave this earth, but it is available to us in the here and now. So why aren't most of us experiencing this life of superabundance Jesus came to give us? One in which we are walking in the fullness of our covenant blessing. One filled with love, joy and peace. Why aren't we seeing the desired fruit in our lives in spite of what seems like our best efforts? Why is it year after year as we acquire more knowledge of the Word of God we see very little change in our lives?

If our post-salvation life looks much the same as our pre-salvation life, with the exception of going to church, praying and reading the Word, then we are missing out on the superabundant life that God has provided for us. Yes, we should do each of these things, but if these actions are not creating any lasting change in our lives we must take some time to consider why. After all if God's Word is true and it always produces a harvest, then there must be a disconnect somewhere. So where is the disconnect?

Our position in life along with our circumstances is a direct reflection of our innermost thoughts. Proverbs 23:7 tells us that as a man thinks in his heart so is he. A man is what he thinks in his heart, not what he thinks in his head. So what does this mean? For purposes of this book, the heart speaks of the subconscious mind, therefore according to Proverbs 23:7, as a man thinks in his subconscious mind so is he.

It has been said 80% of our internal dialogue occurs at the subconscious level, while only 20% occurs at the conscious level. This means at any given moment we are unaware of 80% of what is present in our mind. As we are consumed with the thoughts in our conscious mind, we are ignorant of our hidden subconscious "programs" that govern our behavior. So if these programs are hidden, how do we find them?

It is important to note our soul is comprised of our mind, will and emotions. Our will and emotions are a direct result of what is present in our mind, both conscious and subconscious. One way to begin to identify hidden programs is to take inventory of our emotions. Our feelings serve as an indicator that something isn't right in our soul. Another way is to evaluate our current circumstances in which we are living. We are always drawn in the direction of our most dominant thoughts. If our life is a mess, then our soul is a mess. Our soul is a mess mainly because of the hidden programs in our subconscious mind. Another way to describe our hidden programs is as our "blind spots."

When driving a car, a blind spot describes the area around the vehicle that cannot be directly observed by the driver while at the controls, under existing circumstances.[2] In the area that cannot be seen, may lurk many dangers. We must find ways to eliminate these blind spots, otherwise we may be run off the road or even worse we may crash and burn. It is no different with the blind spots in our lives. If we do not acknowledge we have blind spots and seek to correct them, and we continue to deny their existence and don't seek them out, we cannot reach our desired destination. Not recognizing and addressing our blind spots may cause us to run off into a ditch. Not making the proper adjustments in our lives will keep us stuck or even worse, destroy us and those around us. Thankfully our cars are equipped with mirrors that when adjusted properly can greatly minimize and even remove our blind spots eliminating many hazards on the way to our destination. In our lives, the Word of God acts as our mirror that shows us our blind spots. Once we are aware of the blind spots, we are able to make the necessary adjustments to reach our God given destination.

I submit to you when we aren't living the superabundant life mentioned in John 10:10, it isn't because we don't have enough faith or because God doesn't want to answer our prayers, or any other number of reasons we may come up with, but rather it is due to our blind spots - issues buried deep in our soul preventing us from receiving the Word of God into our heart. We may agree with the Word at a conscious level, but if it isn't producing the intended harvest, it is because something contrary to its purpose is already planted in our heart. True transformation occurs at the heart level.

Romans 12:2 in the New Living Translation says "*...let God transform you into a new person by changing the way you think.*" If we combine the wisdom of Proverbs 23:7 and Romans 12:2 we might say: *Let God transform you into a new person by changing the way you think in your heart.* As Christians our greatest challenge is changing the way we think, not just at the conscious level but more importantly at the heart level. This book will help you transform your thinking by providing an understanding of how hidden beliefs are planted, the damaging effects they have on your life, and how to identify them and how to overcome them.

Right now you may be stuck in a deep pit of despair feeling there is no way out or you may have hit a wall on your journey you cannot climb over or knock down no matter what you do. Whether you are stuck in a pit or have hit a plateau and just can't seem to breakthrough, this book will help get you to the next level and beyond. As a result of reading this book and understanding and applying the principles within, you will be able to identify and overcome obstacles holding you back from the victorious and abundant life you have been missing out on and you will understand how to exchange your thoughts for God's thoughts and embrace your identity in Christ.

This book comes with a companion workbook. I highly recommend you download the workbook from the Diamond Shapers website at www.diamondshapers.com/allaccessworkbook to assist you in applying the principles outlined in this book. You may also wish to consider signing up for the web-based curriculum which will further enhance your experience as I walk you through the content of the book and provide additional insights and instruction. You will also have the opportunity to connect with others participating in the course in a private members only community. Engaging with others will provide additional support and encouragement to you on your journey. You can find the schedule of upcoming course dates at www.diamondshapers.com/classes.

Are you ready to unlock all of God's promises so you can live a life superabundant in quantity and superior in quality? If so, I invite you to join me on a journey of self-discovery that will change the way you think about yourself, God and others and will bring freedom in every area of your life.

Chapter 1

The Soul Battle

15For I do not understand my own actions [I am baffled,
bewildered]. I do not practice or accomplish what I wish,
but I do the very thing that I loathe [which my moral
instinct condemns]. 16Now if I do [habitually] what is
contrary to my desire, [that means that] I acknowledge
and agree that the Law is good (morally excellent) and
that I take sides with it. 17However, it is no longer I who
do the deed, but the sin [principle] which is at home in me
and has possession of me. 18For I know that nothing good
dwells within me, that is, in my flesh. I can will what is
right, but I cannot perform it. [I have the intention and
urge to do what is right, but no power to carry it out.] 19
For I fail to practice the good deeds I desire to do, but the
evil deeds that I do not desire to do are what I am [ever]
doing. 20Now if I do what I do not desire to do, it is no
longer I doing it [it is not myself that acts], but the sin
[principle] which dwells within me ***[fixed and operating***
in my soul]. *21 So I find it to be a law (rule of action of my*
being) that when I want to do what is right and good, evil
is ever present with me and I am subject to its insistent
demands. 22For I endorse and delight in the Law of God in
my ***inmost self [with my new nature].*** *23 But I discern in*
my bodily members [in the sensitive appetites and wills of
the flesh] a different law (rule of action) at war against
the law of my mind (my reason) and making me a
prisoner to the law of sin that dwells in my bodily organs
[in the sensitive appetites and wills of the flesh].
~ Romans 7:15-23 AMP

I suspect most of us have had a dialogue with ourselves similar to the one Paul had with himself in Romans 7. The modern day version might go something like this – *What is wrong with me? Why can't I overcome this issue? Why do I keep making the same poor choices over and over again? I know what God's Word says I should do, but why do I fail when it comes to actually doing it?*

As Christians all too often we know what we are supposed to do, yet we struggle with doing the right thing. Why? Paul's statements in verses 20-22 of Romans 7 shed some light on this universal struggle. As Paul says, the sin principle is fixed and operating in his soul, but his new nature, his regenerated spirit, his inmost self, delights in the Word of God. The moment we accept Jesus Christ as our Lord and Savior we are engaged in a battle – a battle between our soul and our new spirit man.

We have this battle because our spirit is regenerated at the time of salvation, but our soul is not. When we accept Jesus Christ as our Lord and Savior, God fills us with His Holy Spirit, depositing within us everything we will ever need, however, we are unable to tap into all God has placed within us until our soul enters into agreement with the Truth that has been deposited in our regenerated spirit. As our soul holds on to old patterns of behavior and ways of thinking, the key to winning the battle that rages within is renewing our minds with the Word of God so we can be Spirit led.

Sanctification vs. Justification

Although we are justified before God at the time we are saved, we are not yet sanctified. Justification occurs at the time of salvation when a believer enters right standing with God through faith alone. God imparts the gift of righteousness to a believer because of Jesus' sacrifice on the cross. We do not earn or work toward being justified, rather we are justified by faith.[1] Unlike justification which is a one-time event, sanctification is an ongoing process through which we are to be conformed to the image of Christ. Sanctification involves the will of the believer and active participation from the believer and only occurs through the renewing of the mind.

Differentiating Body, Soul & Spirit

Man consists of three parts – body, soul and spirit. The real you is a spirit being that possesses a soul and lives in a physical body. At the time of salvation, the Holy Spirit came to live on the inside of you causing your spirit to be one with His. When the Holy Spirit came to dwell in you, He placed within your spirit everything you need.

> [3] *By his divine power, God has given us everything we need for living a godly life. We have received all of this by coming to know him, the one who called us to himself by means of his marvelous glory and excellence.*
> **~ 2 Peter 1:3 NLT**

It is the Holy Spirit that enables us to walk in the will of God and empowers us to do all He has called us to do. Since God has given us everything we need to live a godly life through His Holy Spirit that resides in us, we do not have to be controlled by our old nature. However, we must learn to be led by the Holy Spirit and we do so by setting our minds on the things of God.

In Romans 8 Paul goes on to say:

> *Therefore, [there is] now no condemnation (no adjudging guilty of wrong) for those who are in Christ Jesus, who live [and] walk not after the dictates of the flesh, but after the dictates of the Spirit. [2] For the law of the Spirit of life [which is] in Christ Jesus [the law of our new being] has freed me from the law of sin and of death. [3] For God has done what the Law could not do, [its power] being weakened by the flesh the entire nature of man without the Holy Spirit]. Sending His own Son in the guise of sinful flesh and as an offering for sin, [God] condemned sin in the flesh subdued, overcame, deprived it of its power over all who accept that sacrifice], [4] So that the righteous and just requirement of the Law might be fully met in us*

who live and move not in the ways of the flesh but in the ways of the Spirit [our lives governed not by the standards and according to the dictates of the flesh, but controlled by the Holy Spirit]. [5]***For those who are according to the flesh and are controlled by its unholy desires set their minds on and pursue those things which gratify the flesh, but those who are according to the Spirit and are controlled by the desires of the Spirit set their minds on and seek those things which gratify the [Holy] Spirit.*** [6]***Now the mind of the flesh [which is sense and reason without the Holy Spirit] is death [death that comprises all the miseries arising from sin, both here and hereafter]. But the mind of the [Holy] Spirit is life and [soul] peace [both now and forever].*** **~ Romans 8:1-6 AMP**

The mind of the flesh is simply a mindset that is in opposition to the truth of God's Word, whereas the mind of the Spirit is in perfect harmony with the Holy Spirit. What we set our mind on determines the results we get in our lives. We cannot set our minds on and pursue the things of the flesh and expect to walk in the promises of God. We must make the choice to set our mind on and seek those things which gratify the Spirit, and allow Him access to our soul so we will be full of life and peace.

To be in perfect harmony we must get our soul in agreement with our regenerated spirit, so the power of the Holy Spirit will flow unhindered from our spirit into our soul and into our body. When we are able to allow His power to flow from our spirit into our soul, our soul prospers and our physical body follows.

[2]*Beloved, I pray that you may prosper in every way and [that your body] may keep well, even as [I know] your soul keeps well and prospers).* **~ 3 John 1:2 AMP**

Our body, soul and spirit all work in tandem with each other with our soul forming the bridge between our spirit and our body.

Therefore, it is our responsibility to get our soul – mind, will and emotions - in alignment with the Holy Spirit God has placed in us. Our soul plays a vital role in our overall well being. Since our soul governs our actions, we must first and foremost be well in our soul to live a victorious life. Unfortunately many Christians today suffer from a sick soul. A sick soul not only affects our spiritual walk, but it also affects our physical health. Many scientific studies have proven the adverse effect our thought life has on our physical bodies.

If we are sick in our soul, we will not prosper in life nor prosper in our health as God has planned for us. The word prosper, as it is used 3 John 1:2, refers to being on the right path leading to real success.[2] Real success is fulfilling God's will for our lives. Romans 12:2 tells us to be transformed by the renewing of our mind so we will know the good, acceptable and perfect will of God. Success starts with a renewed mind.

The Greek word used for soul in 3 John 1:2 is *psyche* and refers to a person's distinct identity.[3] If we have a false identity due to lies buried deep within our soul we will not prosper. We must learn to identify with Christ and embrace our identity in Him. Our soul prospers when we know who we are in Christ and when we fully embrace and walk in that identity.

Feeding Your Spirit

It is important we nourish our spirit with the Word of God. When we feed our spirit with His words, our spirit man grows stronger causing our soul to prosper. Providing nourishment for our spirit man is just as important as providing nourishment for our physical bodies.

> *It has been written, Man shall not live and be upheld and sustained by bread alone, but by every word that comes forth from the mouth of God.* ~ **Matthew 4:4 AMP**

> *Blessed (happy, fortunate, prosperous, and enviable) is the man who walks and lives not in the counsel of the*

> *ungodly [following their advice, their plans and purposes], nor stands [submissive and inactive] in the path where sinners walk, nor sits down [to relax and rest] where the scornful [and the mockers] gather.* ***2But his delight and desire are in the law of the Lord, and on His law (the precepts, the instructions, the teachings of God) he habitually meditates (ponders and studies) by day and by night. 3And he shall be like a tree firmly planted [and tended] by the streams of water, ready to bring forth its fruit in its season; its leaf also shall not fade or wither; and everything he does shall prosper [and come to maturity].*** **~Psalm 1:1-3 AMP**

One day I began to question God as to why I seemed to be struggling and why I was feeling so disconnected. I couldn't put my finger on why I felt so empty and dry. A few days after I began to inquire of the Lord I was reading the book *John G. Lake: The Complete Collection of His Life Teachings.* In one of his sermons he shared a story of a man who had a recurring dream. In the dream the man saw a wilted flower in the desert. The Lord revealed to the man the flower represented his spirit. It was withering and dying. When the man asked the Lord what he needed to do, the Lord replied *"What would you do for a flower in this condition?"* At that moment the man realized just as the flower needed to be cultivated properly, so must his spirit man.[4] Our spirit needs to be watered and fed, just as a flower needs to be watered and fed. Our spirit man drinks from and gets its nourishment from the Word of God.

As I finished reading this story, in my mind I saw an image of a baby sitting in the corner of a dark room, who had been neglected, was severely malnourished and was underdeveloped. The baby's growth was stunted because he had not been given the proper care. I believe the Lord was showing me I had neglected my newborn spirit that was now chronologically a young adult, but was functioning as a malnourished under developed child. When we are born again of the spirit, we must nourish and train our spirit as we would a baby. We do this by feeding on the Word of God through reading the Word and hearing the Word.

I had not spent enough time praying or reading and studying the Word. One reason is I often felt defeated and I didn't believe God would move on my behalf because I wasn't doing enough or performing well enough for Him. I didn't believe He would do for me what He was doing for others because I felt like I could not measure up to His standards. I always felt as though God was disappointed in me, so I pulled away from Him because I didn't think I could be who He wanted me to be or do what He was asking me to do. For years I struggled with an "all or nothing" mentality. One of my favorite things to say was *"If I can't do it exactly right, why bother?"*

When we read the Word of God, we may be reading the words on the page through our mind, but we connect with the Word of God through our spirit. His Spirit and His life connect with our spirit. Although we may mentally acknowledge the Word of God is true, it does not mean we believe it in our heart for ourselves. Unless we truly believe it in our heart, we are unable to receive from God in accordance with His Word. We must remove any wrong ways of thinking that hinder us from receiving.

Unfortunately salvation does not erase wrong ways of thinking. Prior to our salvation we have spent years developing wrong mindsets and bad habits. Not only is our mind filled with wrong beliefs, it is often filled with unbelief, therefore we must begin the work of reprogramming our mind and we do so by studying and meditating on the Word of God.

Many of us have heard amazing testimonies of God healing and delivering people from bondages such as drug, alcohol or tobacco addictions at the time of salvation, but not one new believer has ever walked away with a completely renewed mind. Old ways of thinking and old patterns of behavior are often still active. God rescues us from the bondage and consequences of sin, but He will not renew our minds for us. We must make the choice to renew our minds and take steps towards doing so each day.

I Believe – Help Me Overcome My Unbelief

As Christians we claim to believe the Word of God, yet often we don't act in accordance with the Word because of the battle between our soul and our new spirit. We may mentally acknowledge and agree the Word of God is true, but the Word must be rooted and planted in our heart to the point it shapes our words and governs our actions. Too often in our inner conflict we believe it, yet at the same time we don't believe it. The exchange between Jesus and the father of a demon possessed boy recorded in Mark 9 demonstrates this conflict with which many of us struggle.

> *16 "What is all this arguing about?" Jesus asked. 17 One of the men in the crowd spoke up and said, "Teacher, I brought my son so you could heal him. He is possessed by an evil spirit that won't let him talk. 18 And whenever this spirit seizes him, it throws him violently to the ground. Then he foams at the mouth and grinds his teeth and becomes rigid. So I asked your disciples to cast out the evil spirit, but they couldn't do it." 19 Jesus said to them, "You faithless people! How long must I be with you? How long must I put up with you? Bring the boy to me." 20 So they brought the boy. But when the evil spirit saw Jesus, it threw the child into a violent convulsion, and he fell to the ground, writhing and foaming at the mouth. 21 "How long has this been happening?" Jesus asked the boy's father. He replied, "Since he was a little boy. 22 The spirit often throws him into the fire or into water, trying to kill him. Have mercy on us and help us, if you can." 23 "What do you mean, 'If I can'?" Jesus asked. "Anything is possible if a person believes." 24 The father instantly cried out, "I do believe, but help me overcome my unbelief!"*
> **~Mark 9:16-24 NLT**

The father cries out *"Lord, I believe; help my unbelief!"* after which

Jesus tells him all things are possible to those who believe. He had heard about the miracles performed by Jesus and His disciples and believed Jesus had the power to heal, but when he made his way to Jesus' disciples they failed to cast out the demon. He had watched his son suffer his entire life, so it was almost impossible to believe his son could be made well. I am sure he heard many wonderful testimonies of people getting healed and demons being cast out, but then the disciples were unsuccessful in casting out the demon. The small glimmer of hope the father had must have diminished even more in that moment.

After the disciples failed to cast out the demon, Jesus arrived on the scene and told the people to bring the boy to him. As soon as the evil spirit saw Jesus, it threw the boy to the ground in a seizure. Surely this brought about a crisis of faith. The father brought his child to the one person he believed was his only hope and when the child was brought to Jesus, he fell to the ground in a violent seizure! Perhaps he had one of the most violent seizures ever and appeared worse. Of course the father would have doubts as his child was writhing around on the ground at the feet of Jesus. This is not what he had envisioned!

As the boy began to convulse violently, Jesus did not immediately cast out the demon, instead He asked, *"How long has this been happening?"* Jesus didn't ask the question because He didn't know the answer. He used the question to open up a dialogue with the father to reveal what was in the man's heart. The father responded, *"Have mercy on us and help us if you can."* The response reveals the father was not fully convinced Jesus could deliver the boy. Jesus immediately addressed his unbelief and said, *"What do you mean, If I can?"* Then He said *"Anything is possible if a person believes."* We do not need to ask God "if you can" - we simply need to believe His Word. If His Word says it, He will do it. Healing and deliverance are yours! That is why Jesus came. To receive it you must simply believe it and receive it.

38 How God anointed and consecrated Jesus of Nazareth

with the [Holy] Spirit and with strength and ability and power; how He went about doing good and, in particular, curing all who were harassed and oppressed by [the power of] the devil, for God was with Him. ~ **Acts 10:38 AMP**

[18] The Spirit of the Lord [is] upon Me, because He has anointed Me [the Anointed One, the Messiah] to preach the good news (the Gospel) to the poor; He has sent Me to announce release to the captives and recovery of sight to the blind, to send forth as delivered those who are oppressed [who are downtrodden, bruised, crushed, and broken down by calamity], ~ **Luke 4:18 AMP**

[35] And Jesus went about all the cities and villages, teaching in their synagogues and proclaiming the good news (the Gospel) of the kingdom and curing all kinds of disease and every weakness and infirmity. ~ **Matthew 9:35 AMP**

When we are not receiving from God, we must check ourselves for any unbelief. Unbelief isn't always obvious because it may be supported by underlying false beliefs. We possess many hidden inner beliefs that are in conflict with God's Word, and it is those beliefs which prevent us from fully receiving the Word of God into our hearts and living the abundant life God has promised to us. We must identify and uproot those hidden beliefs lurking beneath the surface that are preventing us from living the abundant life God has prepared for us. Unbelief will keep us from God's best for us just as it did for the Israelites.

The Process

[17]When Pharaoh finally let the people go, God did not lead them along the main road that runs through Philistine territory, even though that was the shortest route to the Promised Land. God said, "If the people are faced with a battle, they might change their minds and return to

> *Egypt." [18]So God led them in a roundabout way through the wilderness toward the Red Sea.* ~ **Exodus 13:17-18 NLT**

Isn't it interesting God never planned to take the Israelites the shortest route to their destination? Although God had given His promise of deliverance to the Israelites He knew at the first sign of trouble they would want to run back to Egypt. He set a path where it would be nearly impossible to backtrack.

Sure enough, when Pharaoh pursued the Israelites they said it would have been better to remain in Egypt than die in the desert.[5] As their journey progresses, the Israelites proclaim this several more times and ultimately the older generation indeed dies in the desert. The Israelites were constantly moved by their circumstances and did not trust God. They praised Him when things were good and grumbled and complained at the first sign of any challenge. They did not keep their minds set on what God had spoken to them.

Often we become frustrated with God, because we feel our journey is taking too long, but He knows what resides in our innermost being and He knows exactly what we need to learn and grow in Him. Because the Israelites had spent so many years in bondage as slaves, they still possessed a slave mentality and they did not yet see themselves as conquerors. Furthermore, they did not have a deep enough understanding of the nature of God and His ways. God knew they were not ready to do battle to march into the Promised Land. He had a purpose in leading them into the wilderness – it was a time of preparation and testing. This was a time for God to reveal Himself to them and allow them to see and experience His faithfulness and His provision. God was using the journey to renew their minds and develop them not only so they would successfully take the Promised Land at the appointed time, but also so they would be able to retain possession of the land once they entered. God desired to change how the Israelites saw Him and how they saw themselves. He knew they were not yet strong enough to handle adversity after 430 years in bondage. Likewise our journey with God always involves preparation for the next stage of life. He will not give us something we are not ready for and He will not ask us to do something we cannot do.

God's Promised Land

> *7 Therefore, as the Holy Spirit says: Today, if you will hear His voice, 8Do not harden your hearts, as [happened] in the rebellion [of Israel] and their provocation and[a]embitterment [of Me] in the day of testing in the wilderness, 9Where your fathers tried [My patience] and tested [My forbearance] and found I stood their test, and they saw My works for forty years. 10And so I was provoked (displeased and sorely grieved) with that generation, and said, They always err and are led astray in their hearts, and* ***they have not perceived or recognized My ways and become progressively better and more experimentally and intimately acquainted with them.*** *11Accordingly, I swore in My wrath and indignation, They shall not enter into My rest.* ***12[Therefore beware] brethren, take care, lest there be in any one of you a wicked, unbelieving heart [which refuses to cleave to, trust in, and rely on Him], leading you to turn away and desert or stand aloof from the living God.*** *13But instead warn (admonish, urge, and encourage) one another every day, as long as it is called Today, that none of you may be hardened [into settled rebellion] by the deceitfulness of sin [by the fraudulence, the stratagem, the trickery which the delusive glamor of his sin may play on him]. 14For we have become fellows with Christ (the Messiah) and share in all He has for us, if only we hold our first newborn confidence and original assured expectation [in virtue of which we are believers] firm and unshaken to the end. 15 Then while it is [still] called Today, if you would hear His voice and when you hear it, do not harden your hearts as in the rebellion [in the desert, when the people provoked and*

> *irritated and embittered God against them]. [16]For who were they who heard and yet were rebellious and provoked [Him]? Was it not all those who came out of Egypt led by Moses? [17]And with whom was He irritated and provoked and grieved for forty years? Was it not with those who sinned, whose dismembered bodies were strewn and left in the desert? [18]And to whom did He swear that they should not enter His rest, but* ***to those who disobeyed*** *[who had not listened to His word and who refused to be compliant or be persuaded]?* ***[19] So we see that they were not able to enter [into His rest], because of their unwillingness to adhere to and trust in and rely on God [unbelief had shut them out].***
> **~ Hebrews 3:7-19 AMP**

God delivered the Israelites from the bondage of Egypt to take them into the Promised Land, but the generation that left Egypt never made it there. Why? This passage of Scripture reveals to us the Israelites did not get to know God and His ways intimately and they were filled with unbelief which kept them out of the Promised Land. To put it simply, their minds were not renewed. It was God's desire to bring them into the Promised Land, but they shut themselves out because of their unbelief. After a two year journey, they were stuck living on the border of the Promised Land for thirty-eight years and eventually died there, although it was never God's will for them to die in the desert. Even after they witnessed God's miraculous intervention for them time and time again, they still did not believe they could possess the land.

God has delivered us out of this world, out from the consequences of sin from the powers of darkness and translated us into the kingdom of his dear Son.[6] The Israelites had to do battle with the enemy in the natural realm to go in and possess their land, and we must do battle with the enemy of our soul to take hold of what God has prepared for us. To do so, we must win the battles raging in our soul. Unbelief and wrong beliefs are a reason we have these soul battles.

Unbelief will shut us out of God's best for us the same way it did for the Israelites. If you only have the ability to believe God for salvation then that is all you will get. God's Word is filled with promises but you must believe those promises are for you to receive those promises. Like the Israelites, we limit God's ability to lead us into His best for us, when we do not trust Him and believe Him. We must choose to discard all of our beliefs that are contrary to His Word and accept all of His Word as truth and act in accordance with His truth. **An unrenewed mind will keep you from the will of God and cause you to miss out on your divine destiny.** An entire generation of Israelites died on the border of God's Promised Land never having experienced God's best for them. If they had truly believed and trusted in God, they would have entered the Promised Land at the time God intended.

Don't allow unbelief and wrong beliefs to keep you wandering in the desert. This is not God's will for you. He has a Promised Land prepared just for you - a special territory He has given to you, but you must be willing to leave the world behind and believe Him and trust Him to take you into your territory to possess the land. God miraculously delivered the Israelites from the bondage of Egypt but the Israelites squandered their freedom. Although they were free from the Egyptians, they died without experiencing God's best for them. Likewise, your unbelief shuts you out of what God has prepared for you. How long have you been camping on the border of what God has for you because of unbelief?

Consequences of Unbelief

Even after the Israelites witnessed God's miraculous provision for two years until they initially reached the border, they still did not believe they could take the Promised Land. When twelve spies were sent in to survey the land, ten of the twelve came back with an "evil report".[7] Joshua and Caleb were the only two of the twelve that came back and said they were well able to take the land.

30But Caleb tried to quiet the people as they stood before Moses. "Let's go at once to take the land," he said. "We can certainly conquer it!" 31But the other men who had explored the land with him disagreed. "We can't go up against them! They are stronger than we are!" 32 So they spread this bad report about the land among the Israelites: "The land we traveled through and explored will devour anyone who goes to live there. All the people we saw were huge. 33 We even saw giants there, the descendants of Anak. Next to them we felt like grasshoppers, and that's what they thought, too!" **~ Numbers 13: 30-31 NLT**

.....

Then the whole community began weeping aloud, and they cried all night. 2Their voices rose in a great chorus of protest against Moses and Aaron. "If only we had died in Egypt, or even here in the wilderness!" they complained.3 "Why is the LORD taking us to this country only to have us die in battle? Our wives and our little ones will be carried off as plunder! Wouldn't it be better for us to return to Egypt?" 4Then they plotted among themselves, "Let's choose a new leader and go back to Egypt! **~ Numbers 14: 1- 5 NLT**

.....

28 Now tell them this: 'As surely as I live, declares the LORD, I will do to you the very things I heard you say. 29 You will all drop dead in this wilderness! Because you complained against me, every one of you who is twenty years old or older and was included in the registration will die. 30 You will not enter and occupy the land I swore to give you. The only exceptions will be Caleb son of Jephunneh and Joshua son of Nun. **~ Numbers 14:28-30 NLT**

The people chose to believe the ten spies who said they were unable to take the land. Because of their unbelief reinforced by their words, God sentenced that generation to remain in the wilderness just outside the Promised Land until they perished. Their negative words coupled with their unbelief resulted in disastrous consequences. Over and over the Israelites said they would die in the wilderness and eventually they did. Only Joshua and Caleb stood in agreement with God as they spoke out to the people they were well able to take the land. Ultimately it was these two men who led the younger generation into the Promised Land.

Connection Between Unbelief & Disobedience

As Christians we know we are called to walk in obedience to God and His Word and we desperately want to be obedient, but too often we fall short and become discouraged. So what exactly prevents us from walking in obedience? If we believe the Word of God to be true, why do we not obey it? Of course, there are many reasons why someone might be disobedient, but I believe one of the main reasons we are often walking in disobedience is because of unbelief constructed of many false beliefs lurking below the surface. Although the desire to obey the Lord and live a life that is holy and consecrated to Him is present, we struggle to do so because of the battles within our soul. To win the battle, we must overcome our unbelief.

> 17*And with whom was He irritated and provoked and grieved for forty years? Was it not with those who sinned, whose dismembered bodies were strewn and left in the desert?* 18*And to whom did He swear that they should not enter His rest, but* ***to those who disobeyed*** *[who had not listened to His word and who refused to be compliant or be persuaded]?* 19*So we see that they were not able to enter [into His rest], because of their unwillingness to adhere to and trust in and rely on God* ***[unbelief had shut them out]****.* **~ Hebrews 3:7-19 AMP**

Verse 18 refers to the Israelites who died in the wilderness as *"those who disobeyed."* When we connect this to verse 19, we come to understand their disobedience was caused by their unbelief. When disobedience is present, unbelief is sustaining it. The Israelites were not fully persuaded God would deliver on His promises.

Isn't it interesting how in some areas obedience seems almost effortless, yet in other areas we are constantly struggling? When there is an area of disobedience, there is something within us preventing us from receiving the Word of God into our heart and allowing us to walk in the fullness of His presence. For myself, in areas where I have great faith, walking in obedience can be easy, but in those areas I struggle with unbelief, obedience is near impossible. Will power is simply not enough.

How do we achieve right behavior? We achieve right actions by first giving our attention to the right thoughts. How was Jesus able to successfully walk in full obedience? Jesus said He could do nothing of Himself. He said and did only what He saw the Father say and do.[8] Jesus was led by the Holy Spirit at all times. Since Jesus is our example, we must determine to become intimately familiar with God and His ways by studying His Word. It is the Word of God that renews our minds and transforms us into His image.

Obedience is a natural byproduct of living a Spirit led life. Rather than being consumed with guilt and condemnation for all of your missteps and being focused on a list of do's and don'ts, instead focus on uprooting false beliefs and renewing your mind with the Word of God, so that you may be led by the Holy Spirit. Using will power to change bad habits or wrong actions rarely works, but changing what you believe will always change your behavior. Right believing always precedes right doing.

The Battles Raging Within

When our mind is not renewed with the truth of God's Word, our soul is in conflict with the Truth of the Holy Spirit that resides in us. A true soul battle goes deeper than a simple struggle between doing right and wrong. In fact, at any given moment, we are fighting multiple battles within our soul. Soul battles are a primary reason why so many of us are walking around angry, frustrated, depressed and defeated.

Many people are unfulfilled and frustrated with their lives. A primary reason for this is because often we are pursuing the wrong things. Some may look to material things for fulfillment or may look to achievement and recognition, while others may look to relationships for validation or to fill a deep void. At the end of the movie *Jerry Maguire,* Jerry tells Dorothy, *"You complete me."* While it sounds quite romantic, it's simply not true. The only one who can complete us is Jesus Christ. A person may complement us well, but they do not complete us. If you are looking to another person to validate your worth and value you will always feel broken and empty. Unfortunately in many instances those with whom we are in relationship with are carrying around their own hidden hurts that are preventing them from being fully present in the relationship. Often their actions cause our insecurities to be reinforced. Likewise, if you are one who seeks your worth and value in achievement, you will continue to feel empty and unfulfilled.

In a teaching by Betsey Kylstra of Restoring the Foundations ministry, she shares a story of a particular "soul battle" she uncovered operating in her life. After being adopted, Betsey struggled with deep feelings of not belonging and she was constantly seeking affirmation even though her adoptive parents were very loving. As an adult working in ministry, she struggled with jealousy, competition and rejection particularly concerning women of similar age who possessed similar gifting. She knew her feelings of jealously and competition were wrong, and she would often pray about her feelings and she would pray for the success of others in an effort to overcome, but she never could get past her feelings and experience true joy within herself or towards others. One day as she was seeking the Lord, He showed her an event from her past.

Over the years, Betsey was often elected by her peers to serve in leadership positions, from president of her brownie troop to captain of her basketball team. Receiving recognition from others made her feel valuable. Her senior year in high school she ran for student council. In Betsey's mind, winning the election would just be one more accomplishment to add to her lengthy list. Unfortunately Betsey lost the election to another girl. Betsey was devastated. The defeat caused her to feel shame and humiliation. She felt rejected and she didn't feel valued. However, it appeared to others as if she had shrugged it off and she never shared her feelings with anyone.

After the Lord reminded her of this event, she asked Him to help her work through this hurt. He said to her *"I love you too much to let you get your value and worth out of elections. I want you to get your validation in Me."* Betsey had believed a lie she was only worthy and accepted when she won. In this moment Betsey chose to receive the love of the Lord and His truth about her. After that encounter, Betsey was free from those feelings that had plagued her for years.[9]

When we experience some type of hurt or defeat our soul may seek to right the wrong or fill the void that was created. The problem with this is the harder we try to fill the void, the more we fail, and the more defeated we become as our soul is constantly fighting the same battle over and over again. We must come to realize we cannot win the battle, but rather we must give the battle to the Lord and allow Him to do the necessary healing in our hearts and minds. We have all heard the saying 'time heals all wounds' and it sounds good, but it's not true. If that is true why are so many wounded people walking around? Time does not heal all wounds, only Jesus does!

What "Lies" Beneath

For years I struggled in my walk with God until I got a revelation of several things buried deep within my soul. Identifying lies I believed about God, myself and others was very freeing and God continues to reveal to me issues hidden in my soul. He has taught me to be aware of my reactions to people and situations as part of the process.

Our responses reveal quite a bit about what is going on deep within our souls, but too often we are running on autopilot unaware of what is bubbling beneath the surface. Rather than praying for God to change us, we pray for Him to change our circumstances and to change those around us. God isn't as interested in changing our circumstances as He is in changing us from the inside out. It is through our circumstances and our relationships that God reveals those areas of *our* character that must be refined.

When you notice a negative or destructive pattern operating in your life, you can almost bet it is because of a hidden soul battle. Soul battles are often based on lies we believe about ourselves, God and others or a combination of all three. These battles occur because of hurts we have experienced in our lives, particularly in childhood, which caused us to develop false beliefs. Too often we are fighting old battles.

If you notice the same pattern occurring in your relationships, guess what? The only constant is Y-O-U! You must take responsibility for your part in every situation. You may not be able to control what others say or do, but you get to choose how you respond. Regardless of what others say or do, you can take steps to improve every relationship by changing your behavior. Your behavior is changed when you change your beliefs.

To live in freedom, we must be able to identify the battles in our soul and we must surrender them to God and allow him to heal our hurts and replace any false beliefs residing within us with the truth of God's Word. To do so, we must submit our minds to the Word of God and submit ourselves to the power of the Holy Spirit. We need to allow His power to flow into souls so we can operate in accordance with His leading.

Choose to see as Jesus sees. Choose to speak as Jesus speaks. Choose to love as Jesus loves.

Chapter 2

No More Excuses

2 Now there is in Jerusalem a pool near the Sheep Gate. This pool in the Hebrew is called Bethesda, having five porches (alcoves, colonnades, doorways). 3 In these lay a great number of sick folk—some blind, some crippled, and some paralyzed (shriveled up)—waiting for the bubbling up of the water. 4 For an angel of the Lord went down at appointed seasons into the pool and moved and stirred up the water; whoever then first, after the stirring up of the water, stepped in was cured of whatever disease with which he was afflicted. 5 There was a certain man there who had suffered with a deep-seated and lingering disorder for thirty-eight years. 6 When Jesus noticed him lying there [helpless], knowing that he had already been a long time in that condition, He said to him, Do you want to become well? [Are you really in earnest about getting well?] 7 The invalid answered, Sir, I have nobody when the water is moving to put me into the pool; but while I am trying to come [into it] myself, somebody else steps down ahead of me. 8 Jesus said to him, Get up! Pick up your bed (sleeping pad) and walk! 9 Instantly the man became well and recovered his strength and picked up his bed and walked. But that happened on the Sabbath. 10 So the Jews kept saying to the man who had been healed, It is the Sabbath, and you have no right to pick up your bed [it is not lawful]. 11 He answered them, The Man Who healed

me and gave me back my strength, He Himself said to me, Pick up your bed and walk! [12] *They asked him, Who is the Man Who told you, Pick up your bed and walk?* [13] *Now the invalid who had been healed did not know who it was, for Jesus had quietly gone away [had passed on unnoticed], since there was a crowd in the place.* [14] *Afterward, when Jesus found him in the temple, He said to him, See, you are well! Stop sinning or something worse may happen to you.* [15] *The man went away and told the Jews that it was Jesus Who had made him well.* ~ **John 5: 2-15 AMP**

One afternoon as I was reading my Bible, I became captivated by this story and I began to ponder the deeper significance of this brief encounter in Scripture. In John 5, we are never specifically told what is wrong with the man at the pool of Bethesda, however it is usually assumed he was suffering from some sort of paralysis or was crippled in some other way. As I began to dig into various translations of this story and began to study the meaning of the Greek words used in the original text, it became apparent to me this story was not about a physical healing, but was about another kind I had not heard of nor considered before.

Several different words and phrases are used to describe the man across the many translations: impotent, had an infirmity, being in ailment, and an invalid, but nothing specific is mentioned about his condition and he is not specifically described as being paralyzed; we only know Jesus finds him lying on a mat beside the pool. So what exactly was his infirmity? What exactly was this deep seated and lingering disorder he suffered with for thirty-eight years? Most readers assume he was paralyzed because of the context of the entire passage, but Scripture does not specifically tell us he suffered from a physical paralysis.

As I read this story over and over again while digging into the Greek translations, I got the impression this man's problem was not so much a physical one, but perhaps a mental one - it appeared to me he had a sick soul. We tend to assume verse 3 is speaking of physical ailments, but my study of the words used in this passage and their context revealed the blind, lame and paralyzed people, could be described as spiritually blind, spiritually lame and spiritually paralyzed due to a sick soul.

Let's take a closer look at this passage verse by verse.

> [3] *In these lay a great number of sick folk—some blind, some crippled, and some paralyzed (shriveled up)—waiting for the bubbling up of the water.* ~ **John 5:3 AMP**

In the original text, the sick people were described as without strength.[1] The Greek word for blind used in this passage is *tuphlos* which refers to being blind physically *or* mentally.[2] Additionally, the word paralyzed literally means dry or withered.[3] Crippled as used in this verse refers to limping.[4] Several of the people at the pool were limping along in life, barely getting by as their souls were dry and parched, weary and worn out. I am not suggesting the people at the pool did not suffer from any physical ailments, rather I am suggesting this story holds some hidden truths for us about our soul and how a sick soul can affect us physically.

The condition of our soul has a profound effect on our body because we are how we perceive ourselves to be. Our thoughts are very powerful. Sometimes our suffering is caused due to what we are thinking as we choose to focus on what is wrong with us, rather than what is right with us. It seems this man was focused on his shortcomings and believed he was weak and defeated. Perhaps he had a setback or small injury causing him to no longer feel like a man. If we no longer view ourselves as capable, then we slowly become incapable.

> [4] *For an angel of the Lord went down at appointed seasons into the pool and moved and stirred up the water; whoever then first, after the stirring up of the water, stepped in was cured of whatever disease with which he was afflicted.* ~ **John 5:4 AMP**

The Greek word used for disease in verse 4 is *nósēma* which means "sickness" but it refers to a chronic illness in terms of its results, especially mental torment.[5] This context alters the picture of those at the pool - people there were suffering not just from physical afflictions, but some were suffering from mental torment associated with various conditions.

For the man at the pool of Bethesda, I believe it wasn't so much a physical cause for his inability to walk, as it was a mental affliction. He had some minor ailment that had taken away his confidence or perhaps at one time he was fully functional but had endured something that caused him to be operating with a handicap. Perhaps something traumatic had occurred stripping him of all of his self confidence. Maybe he had endured some injustice or injury as a child at the hand of his parents or some other trusted authority figure. Maybe he was told by others he was incapable or unworthy. Maybe he had stepped out into his destiny and he was smacked down by some unfortunate circumstance. Life didn't go how he had planned. Life treated him unfairly. We don't know his age - we only know he had suffered for thirty-eight years.

> 5 *There was a certain man there who had suffered with a* ***deep-seated*** *and* ***lingering disorder*** *for thirty-eight years.* ~ **John 5:5 AMP**

The Amplified Bible describes the man as one who had suffered with a *"deep seated and lingering disorder."* The word lingering indicates something has the potential to leave, yet does not. Physical paralysis is rarely temporary. In fact, during this period of time, before the advances of modern medicine, I suspect paralysis was almost always a permanent condition.

The *"lingering disorder"* was described as *"deep-seated."* This phraseology is often associated with something being "deep seated in the soul". Just as physical paralysis would not be described as lingering, neither would it be described as deep-seated, however, mental anguish is often referred to as deep-seated or lingering. As you learned in Chapter 1, many of our struggles are firmly fixed and rooted in our soul. When we are wounded in our soul we are weak and ineffective and we are unable to live a productive life. This man had lost his strength and he was not enjoying his life. He was stuck.

In the original text the man is described as an invalid using the Greek word *asthéneia* which literally means "without strength" and refers to *"an ailment that deprives someone of enjoying or accomplishing what they would like to do."* Furthermore it, *"expresses the weakening influences of the illness or a particular problem, especially as someone becomes wrongly (overly) dependent."*[6] We see evidence in verse 6, the man had indeed become overly dependent on others when Jesus asked the man if he wanted to get well. Rather than answering the question directly the man responded he had no one to help him into the pool.

> 6 *When Jesus noticed him lying there [helpless], knowing that he had already been a long time in that condition, He said to him, Do you want to become well? [Are you really in earnest about getting well?]* 7 *The invalid answered, Sir, I have nobody when the water is moving to put me into the pool; but while I am trying to come [into it] myself, somebody else steps down ahead of me.* 8 *Jesus said to him, Get up! Pick up your bed (sleeping pad) and walk!*
> 9 *Instantly the man became well and recovered his strength and picked up his bed and walked. But that happened on the Sabbath.* ~ **John 5:6-9 AMP**

There was certainly more to this man's affliction than met the eye. Why did Jesus approach the man in the manner He did asking him "*do you want to become well?*" It was because when Jesus saw the man sitting by the pool, He perceived what was in his heart. Jesus was asking him *"do you really want to get well?"* The Greek word *thélō* is used here which means to desire. Specifically it refers to "*wanting what is best (optimal) because someone is ready and willing to act and it is commonly used of the Lord extending His "best-offer" to the believer wanting (desiring) to birth His persuasion (faith) in them which also empowers, and manifests His presence."* [7]

Jesus is saying to the man– *I want what is best for you. Are you ready and willing to act?* Jesus will always call us to action. What does He ask us to do? He simply asks us to believe in Him – to trust Him, to rely on Him, to rest in Him. The man had to believe he could do what Jesus told him to do otherwise he wouldn't have gotten up. He easily could have continued to sit there, but there was something different about his conversation with Jesus than those conversations he had with others. Jesus didn't take pity on him or feel sorry for him. That would have simply reinforced the man's issue. Instead Jesus ignored his excuses and challenged him. How many people had enabled this man all of his life? Pity certainly didn't serve him well. It made him overly dependent on those around him. He became comfortable with his situation. The man probably expected pity from Jesus, but instead Jesus gave him a command. Jesus did not reinforce his current state, but challenged him to rise up and transition himself into a new state of being.

> [8] *Jesus said to him, Get up! Pick up your bed (sleeping pad) and walk!* ~ **John 5:8 AMP**

The Greek word for walk is *peripatéō* which means *"I walk, I conduct my life"*. It means to walk around in a complete circuit i.e. going "full circle."[8] When Jesus told him to get up and walk, He wasn't just telling him to get up off of his mat, but He was commanding him to get up and start living his life and living it to the full. Jesus was saying to him, *"You have been stuck long enough. Get up and walk it out! You are well able."*

After his encounter with Jesus the man was walking around in the temple carrying his mat.

> [14] *Afterward, when Jesus found him in the temple, He said to him, See, you are well! Stop sinning or something worse may happen to you.* [15] *The man went away and told the Jews that it was Jesus Who had made him well.* ~ **John 5:14-15 AMP**

The word used for see is *horáō* which means to properly see. It is often used metaphorically to see with the mind or perceive with inward spiritual perception.[9] This indicates the man was limited in his mind, not by his physical condition. Jesus was reiterating to the man he was well. Jesus wanted him to see and believe through his mind that he really was well. It seems to me Jesus was really saying, *"Don't you see?? You ARE well!! All you had to do was get up and walk!"*

In the original text, Jesus says "see you have become well." The word used for "have become" in the original text is *gínomai* which means to transition from one realm, condition or state or place to another.[10] Jesus also told the man he had become *hugiés*, which means sound or whole, referring to being well in physical body, but it also refers to being true in doctrine which simply put can be described as right believing![11] We are whole when we possess sound doctrine which is being fully persuaded of each and every truth presented in the Word of God.

In verse 14, when Jesus reiterated to the man that he was well, he admonished him to stop sinning so something worse would not happen to him. So what exactly was this man's sin? Scripture does not reveal that to us, but I believe this man's sin was the sin of self-pity and allowing a victim mentality to take up residence in his mind keeping him in bondage for thirty-eight years. Jesus was warning him not to fall back into old mindsets and old ways. We must think about what we are thinking about and be careful not to allow negative self defeating thoughts to take up residence in our minds.

At the temple the Jews questioned the man about who told him to pick up his mat and walk.

> *10 So the Jews kept saying to the man who had been healed, It is the Sabbath, and you have no right to pick up your bed [it is not lawful].* ~ **John 5:10 AMP**

The religious leaders told the man he had no right to be healed! I can imagine some of the things they might have said to him: *Who do you think you are? You're just a disabled beggar. You do not belong here walking around in the temple. Go back to the pool where you belong. You should not be here. You are breaking the law. You are not worthy.*

When you experience freedom there are many religious folks who won't like it. They will do their best to convince you to go back to your prior state, because your transition makes them uncomfortable with themselves as it forces them to call into question their own beliefs they hold so dear. Do not allow these people to talk you out of God's blessing for you!

Do You Really Want to Get Well?

When Jesus initially approached the man He asked him *"Do you want to get well?"* At first that seems like such a peculiar question for Jesus to ask. You might think *'Of course he does Jesus. What kind of question is that? Why else would he keep hanging out at the pool?'* Obviously Jesus perceived something about this man beyond his physical appearance.

Almost as peculiar as Jesus' question, so is the man's response to Jesus. Rather than saying *'Yes! I want to be well. I'll do whatever it takes.'* He responds (paraphrase), *"Sir, I have no one to put me into the pool. When I am trying to get in someone else gets in ahead of me."* As I read these words I can hear the man responding to Jesus in a whiny tone of voice filled with self-pity.

The man claimed he had no one to put him into the pool, but how did the man get to the pool in the first place? Surely he didn't sit at the pool all day every day year after year. Somehow he managed to get to the edge of the pool, but he always fell short of actually getting in the pool. In his words to Jesus he blamed others for him not being well. He told Jesus he had no one to help him into the pool and that others came and pushed him out of the way before he could get in to receive his healing. The fact is this man knew exactly what he needed to do - he needed to be at the pool at a certain time and he needed to be the first one in to get healed.

I believe the man had resigned himself to the limitations of his condition and he became settled in his condition. It was familiar. He was comfortable not taking responsibility for himself and playing on the sympathy of others around him. Each opportunity that passed him by he chose to be a victim rather than to walk in victory. I am sure he was miserable, but rather than taking action he relied on the occasional kindness of others to carry him through his existence.

So back to the question at hand, how did the man get to the pool? Either he somehow made it to the pool on his own or someone helped him get to the pool. Assuming he made it to the pool on his own, he should have been able to get into the pool on his own if he had some means of mobilization, but maybe he couldn't make it to the pool on his own. Perhaps he had someone who felt sorry for him and carried him to the pool each time and set him down on the porch so he could sit and beg for food and money while he waited for the stirring of the waters.

Whichever way he made it to the pool, I am convinced for thirty-eight years this man was surrounded by people who enabled him to remain in his condition. After all, his healing was in front of him the whole time. I think all of those years the man was physically capable, but in his mind he had convinced himself he was not. Why do I think that? Because this man didn't even know who Jesus was when Jesus told him to pick up his mat and walk. It had nothing to do with his faith in Jesus. As far as this man was concerned Jesus was just another man who happened to stop and have a conversation with him.

When the man answered Jesus, he blamed others for his remaining in his condition and for his not being healed. He was not willing to take responsibility for his own inaction; rather he placed the responsibility on those around him. In reality, the only person standing in the way of the man's healing was the man himself. The man wasn't really serious about getting well. His victim mentality and his dependence on others kept him crippled.

There are some things only we can do that we cannot rely on others to do for us. All it took for the man to be made whole was being obedient to the words of Jesus. He didn't need anyone or anything else to be made well. Rather than sitting around waiting for circumstances to be perfect, or for others to do things for us, we must get up and do what we can with what we have. If we choose to linger by the pool, nothing will change. We hinder God's power in our lives when we do so. We must cooperate with God. God wants us to get up and walk – walk with Him!

I have to wonder, did anyone else around this man ever tell him to pick up his mat and walk? Probably not. Perhaps they fed into his victim mentality. Many of those around him may have been comfortable with him being an invalid. Jesus perceived exactly what this man needed to hear. It was indeed a divine appointment to walk into his destiny. Thank God he chose to get up and walk, instead of spending another thirty-eight years lingering by the pool! He chose to be well.

Unfortunately, some people don't want to "get well." You might know of a family member or a friend who doesn't want to "get well." Or maybe it's you who doesn't want to "get well." As crazy as it may sound there are some people who do not want to get well. Too many people have allowed their affliction to become their identity!

Have you ever known a person who has some disease or illness and all they do is talk about their disease or illness? For some people their entire life revolves around their sickness. It becomes their identity because they are seeking what comes along with it – the attention, the sympathy, the pity. The man at the pool probably had resigned himself to his current state of defeat, and at the same time he used it to his advantage to play on the sympathy of others. He defined himself by his affliction.

Many people do not have a physical illness, but they continually talk about how they were hurt or wronged by others in the past. Usually they are looking for pity and sympathy. Playing the role of the victim is comfortable for them. They take advantage of the kindness and compassion of others, not wanting to take full responsibility for themselves. After all, as long as they are the victim of their circumstances and of others, then they do not need to take responsibility for their own actions.

Others may allow themselves to be defined by their past mistakes, living with much regret and condemnation. Regardless of the scenario, each one keeps us in bondage - spiritually paralyzed like the man at the pool of Bethesda.

Location, Location, Location

In real estate the phrase location, location, location is often used to emphasize the importance of physical location, but more important than your physical location, is your mental and spiritual location. First, you must have the right spiritual location – justification which comes through receiving salvation by faith. Justification places you in right standing with God. Second, your soul must be in its proper location, rooted and grounded in the Word of God through a renewed mind. Your intended destination is of little importance if you don't have the correct mental map to get there. You will never arrive at your God ordained destination until you clear your path of all of the hindrances in your way. Whining, wishing and hoping won't get you anywhere. You must take action.

In John 5, the physical location was the pool of Bethesda, but the man's physical location had not done him any good. He was in the right place at the right time, but nothing happened. Why? He didn't take action. He was unable to complete what was required of him. Perhaps he didn't want to or perhaps he didn't believe he could. Jesus asked him if he really wanted to get well so the man would realize his location mentally. Jesus perceived exactly what the man needed to hear. After hearing the man's excuses, Jesus simply issued him a command. He didn't stop to have a pity party with him. When God speaks a word to us, very often a corresponding action is required on our part. We must cooperate with Him, otherwise we will stay in a holding pattern.

You can be in the right place at the right time, but if you take no action, there will be no change. However, if you are in the wrong place at the wrong time, you can create change by taking action. It's not so much where you are at, but what you are doing where you are at. It is important to make the most of every set of circumstances. The man at the pool had an internal battle, a soul battle that held him back. The man didn't suffer from lack of knowing what to do, but rather from not doing it.

The Holy Spirit will ask us a question to assist us in locating where we are at spiritually. Jesus never asked a question because He didn't know the answer, rather He asked questions for the benefit of those He was teaching. After Adam and Eve hid from God in the Garden of Eden, God called out, *"Adam where are you?".* God knew exactly where Adam was and what had happened. [12] God used the question to open up a dialogue between Himself and Adam. It is in this dialogue Adam confesses fear and shame over his disobedience. But even in their disobedience we see God's mercy on Adam and Eve.

The man was on the edge of the pool several times, but he never did take the plunge. Apparently others wanted it more because they were willing to push forward to get in the pool. I imagine the scene at the pool was filled with anticipation. People crowding around perhaps camping out days in advance for a chance to get into the water and be healed. People were probably pushing and shoving each other out of the way and knocking each other down to be the first into the pool as the angel of the Lord came down to stir the waters.

To describe this part of the story in modern terms, I picture a scene similar to a black Friday stampede at Wal-Mart or Best Buy with people pushing and shoving and trampling others in their quest to get the latest electronics in limited quantities at rock bottom prices. This got me to thinking, why is it many will fight and claw for material possessions, but rarely will fight for their spiritual and mental well being? After all, what is more valuable? God has provided everything we need to live an abundant life aside from material possessions. Shouldn't we spend our time pursuing all He has for us?

I suppose if someone came up to you and handed you a blank check or a credit card without limit, told you to go out and get whatever you wanted and you did not have to pay the bill, you would not have such a difficult time going on a huge shopping spree. The good news is we have something better. Jesus paid the ultimate price for us. He paid the price for our sin with His own life. He came so we could have life and have it more abundantly, yet we do not lay claim to it. God has given us His best offer. We need to grab hold of everything He has promised us in His Word.

Excuses, Excuses

Have you ever encountered someone who had an excuse for everything? Someone who whined and complained about life, yet when any advice was offered about what to do to change the situation they countered it with an excuse? Maybe you are that person. These people frustrate me. Don't get me wrong I have been guilty of it myself from time to time, but the further I move away from making excuses and getting really honest with myself, the more it gets under my skin when people do this. I am talking about those who *always* have a reason for not taking action regardless of what is presented to them. Rather than searching for ways something can work, they are always coming up with reasons why it won't work. Most reasons are not reasons, rather they are excuses.

I challenge you to look at the excuses you are making on a regular basis because **behind every excuse is a false belief.** It may be a false belief about yourself, others, God or a combination of all three. When Jesus asked the man at the pool if he really wanted to get well, he didn't answer with a yes or no, he replied with an excuse. Jesus knew up until that moment he hadn't been serious about getting well.

Many people went to the pool for healing, but only one was healed – the first. Perhaps the man started out whole heartedly seeking to get into the pool, but he had suffered defeat so many times he had given up hope and he was just going through the motions. I wonder how many times he came to the pool during those years. We don't know how long he was at the pool, only that he had suffered thirty-eight years.

Sometimes we perceive we cannot when we can. Sometimes our circumstances remain the same for so long we do not believe anything can change or will change. We feel we are too far gone. We feel so defeated we can't muster up enough strength to lift ourselves up. We are afraid of failure. We are afraid of falling again.

During my recovery after my lengthy illness, I kept telling myself I couldn't do certain things because my illness had taken a great toll on my physical body. In reality I was capable of many things, but I made myself believe I was not. When people would suggest to me that I should start doing certain things, I would quickly shut them down and give a list of reasons as to why I could not do them. I was simply making excuses for things I didn't really want to do, but as I gradually started to return to certain activities, I realized I had been fully capable for quite some time, but in my mind I hadn't believed I was ready. Looking back, I was waiting on the miraculous, and was not willing to do my part.

People always talk about waiting on God, but I think more often God is waiting on us. He is waiting for us to believe Him. That is our part in appropriating the promises of God - simply to believe Him. We cease from our own labors and enter the rest of God when we trust Him and rely on Him fully. When we allow ourselves to wallow in self-pity or play the role of victim we are saying people are more powerful than God and our circumstances are greater than our God. When we allow ourselves to wallow in rejection we are saying what others think about us is more powerful than what God says about us. When we allow shame to control us we are saying shame is more powerful than God and we are beyond repair and we negate God's grace. When we allow fear to control us we are saying we do not trust God.

We live in a broken world full of broken people. People are paralyzed because of fear, shame, guilt, rejection, unworthiness – not just unbelievers, but believers. Too many have bought into the lies of the enemy. We are to be Spirit led, yet many of us are ruled by our soul, living our lives as carnal Christians. This ought not to be. We spend our days doing our will and not His because we are in bondage to our own false beliefs.

Grace & Mercy

A detail often overlooked in the story of the man at the pool, is the significance of the name of the pool and the number of porches at the pool. Each one reveals something about the nature of God.

In Hebrew, Bethesda means "house of mercy" or "flowing water" and the number five is the number for grace and favor in Hebrew.[13,14] The pool of Bethesda is literally a reservoir of flowing water filled with God's grace and mercy. It is a place symbolic of where grace and mercy collide – where healing waters flow. The healing the man experienced was realized because of God's grace and mercy extended to him through Jesus. The man was not healed because of his faith; he didn't even know who Jesus was! It was the grace and mercy of our Lord at work with this man's infirmity during the brief encounter. Jesus sought him out among the multitudes.

We are always surrounded by God's grace and mercy, but we don't immerse ourselves in it – we don't fully surrender and jump in. We disqualify ourselves. This might be because of fear or because we have bought into the lies the enemy of our soul has whispered into our ear through those around us - parents, siblings, authority figures, etc. convincing us we are unworthy. Or maybe we are our own worst enemy as we become self sabotaging and self defeating, wallowing in a victim mentality and manipulating others into doing things we aren't willing to do for ourselves.

How many of us make it into the church and to the edge of the pool, but never actually have the courage to jump in? Do not allow yourself to become complacent and wallow in self pity. Stop blaming others, lay down all excuses and jump into the pool. Jesus is waiting! Get up and walk! Walk according to His Word and jump into His pool to receive all He has for you.

Believe You Can

You might be wondering why I devoted an entire chapter to the story of the man at the pool of Bethesda. This story spoke to me in the summer of 2012, the summer I was turning thirty-eight. Although I had experienced a degree of healing both physically and mentally over the prior year, I still found myself making excuses for why I could not do what God was calling me to do. I didn't feel I was ready. I believed I was not able to do what needed to be done. Just like the man at the pool, I had spent thirty-eight years of my life lingering around, not having the courage to step out into what God was calling me to do. I felt the Lord was telling me – *Get up and walk! Get up and do what you know you need to do. Stop sitting around and making excuses. You are well able!*

If you are sitting on the sidelines, you are robbing others of the gifts God has placed within you. If you need help, seek help. It doesn't matter what you have or haven't done – no matter how awful, and it doesn't matter what others have said about you or done to you. What matters is you get up every day and walk – put one foot in front of the other and keep taking steps toward the destiny God has for you. Do not become comfortable in your mess. Do not be ashamed. What you do does not define who you are – God defines you. Learn to embrace who God says you are and know who you are in Christ. Let your mess become your message bringing freedom to yourself and others.

Henry Ford is credited with saying "*Whether you believe you can or you can't you are right.*" I am challenging you to believe you can. Believe you can fulfill God's plan for your life and believe you can live the abundant life Jesus died to give you. You are well able. You are an overcomer because of what Jesus did for you on the cross. You have no *legitimate* excuse for living a defeated life.

> [10] *The thief comes only in order to steal and kill and destroy. I came that they may have and enjoy life, and have it in abundance (to the full, till it overflows).* **~ John 10:10 AMP**

> [33] *I have told you these things, so that in Me you may have [perfect] peace and confidence. In the world you have tribulation and trials and distress and frustration; but be of good cheer [take courage; be confident, certain, undaunted]! For I have overcome the world. [I have deprived it of power to harm you and have conquered it for you.]* **~ John 16:33 AMP**

> [37] *Yet amid all these things we are more than conquerors and gain a surpassing victory through Him Who loved us.* **~ Romans 8:37 AMP**

Many of us are lying around on our mats not living the life God has purposed for us. We cannot look to others to do for us what God is calling us to do ourselves. We have to lay down all of our excuses, our complacency and get up and walk it out. No matter how defeated you may feel, God is calling you to get up and walk! Life may have knocked you down, but you need to get up and walk. First walk, then run. Run the race God has set before you. It doesn't matter how you start, it only matters how you finish. Decide to finish strong. Clear those obstacles in your path and run your race. It is my hope the truth in this book will set you free to get up and walk.

Maybe as you read this you're afraid to "get up and walk" – *what if I fall? What if people laugh at me? What if people reject me?* Well, what is the alternative? Spending another year lingering on the edge of the pool? Another year settling for the status quo? Jesus gave His life so you could have an abundant life; not one of sitting on the sidelines as a victim of circumstance. Don't insult the gift and its Giver by not fully embracing it. Don't squander the gift!!

What in life has knocked you down? What has caused you to give up? What would happen if you took action? What wrong ways of thinking have been keeping you in bondage? Have you become comfortable in your mess? Are you afraid to take responsibility for yourself and your choices? Are you afraid to step out? This book will help you understand why and will assist you in rising above and stepping out into all God has for you.

Chapter 3

Renewing the Mind

I appeal to you therefore, brethren, and beg of you in view of [all] the mercies of God, to make a decisive dedication of your bodies [presenting all your members and faculties] as a living sacrifice, holy (devoted, consecrated) and well pleasing to God, which is your reasonable (rational, intelligent) service and spiritual worship. 2Do not be conformed to this world (this age), [fashioned after and adapted to its external, superficial customs], but be transformed (changed) by the [entire] renewal of your mind [by its new ideals and its new attitude], so that you may prove [for yourselves] what is the good and acceptable and perfect will of God, even the thing which is good and acceptable and perfect [in His sight for you]. ~ **Romans 12:1-2 AMP**

The primary purpose of renewing our minds is so we can know the perfect will of God for our lives and walk in it. Since the Word of God is His will for man, the only way we can know His will for us and present ourselves holy and well pleasing to God is by renewing our mind with the Word of God. Renewing the mind is the key to winning the battles in our soul.

Renewing the Mind – What Does It Mean?

Most of us have realized by now, using sheer will power to implement permanent and lasting change in our lives doesn't work.

Yes, making a change involves our will, because we must first make a choice to change, but the only way to permanently change our behavior and change our lives is to change the way we think. In fact, Romans 12:2 in the New Living Translation says "*...let God transform you into a new person by changing the way you think...*"

I strongly believe there should be a required course called Christianity 101: Renewing the Mind because the lines are often blurred between believers and non-believers. In many ways Christians aren't behaving any differently than non-believers, nor are many walking in victory as the Word of God promises. The root cause is an unrenewed mind.

So what exactly does it mean to "renew the mind"? This phrase left me scratching my head for years. I heard it hundreds of times, but never really understood it. I heard many preachers and teachers say to their audience "you need to renew your mind with the Word of God", but the messages would always stop there. I think when most of us hear this we think it simply means we need to read our Bible more. While that is a critical element of renewing the mind, in order to grasp this concept fully, we must first understand the desired outcome of this process.

A few years ago I was reading the book *Transform Your Thinking, Transform Your Life* by Dr. Bill Winston. As I was reading a simple illustration he used about having a renewed mind, I became so excited because I finally understood what it meant to have a renewed mind. He compared renewing the mind with learning how to ride a bike. When we get on a bicycle for the first time all of our focus is on riding the bike. When we are on the bike we aren't focused on anything except doing what we need to do to keep from falling over and injuring ourselves. We aren't thinking about anything else in that moment other than what we need to do to keep the bike up and moving. But eventually we learn to ride the bike and it becomes second nature to us. We get to the point where we can ride the bike without even thinking about it. We don't need to go through a mental checklist of how to get on the bike and what we need to do to keep from falling over - we just get on the bike and ride without ever giving a thought to how we are doing it.[1]

After I read this illustration I also thought about how it was similar to learning how to drive a car. At first we may feel overwhelmed with everything involved in driving a car, but eventually we get to the point when we are driving a car we aren't consciously thinking about what we need to do or how we need to do it to get where we are going.

Have you ever driven a distance in your car, reached your destination and then realized your mind had been on something else the entire drive? We have all been there! Although our conscious mind may have been preoccupied with our to-do list or an argument we may have had earlier that day, our subconscious mind was able to carry out the function of driving for us and get us to where we needed to go. Both driving a car and riding a bike become second nature to us. We are able to carry out each of these activities automatically, never thinking about the individual steps involved as we are doing the activity.

Sometimes when I am outside of my normal routine on a particular day, as I get lost in thought I am running on auto-pilot. I automatically turn left when leaving my home, because that is what I do every morning, but I need to turn right because I have a different plan for that day. My internal programming brought about by repetition guides my actions when my conscious mind is preoccupied.

So how does this relate to a renewed mind? Just as these activities become second nature to us, certain behaviors and actions should also become second nature to us. We are instructed to renew our mind with the Word of God so His thoughts and words will become second nature to us enabling us to automatically think and act like Him. What a revelation for me! The goal is to be so full of God's Word no matter where I am, no matter what I am doing, no matter what happens I can automatically act in accordance with God's will and

His Word without even thinking about how or what to do. It will flow naturally! When we renew our mind and exchange our thoughts and ideas for God's thoughts and ideas He has provided in His Word, we will be transformed and be walking in the perfect will of God for our lives.

Let's take a closer look at our foundational scripture in Romans 12:2 (AMP):

> *"Do not be conformed to this world (this age), [fashioned after and adapted to its external, superficial customs], but be transformed (changed) by the [entire] renewal of your mind [by its new ideals and its new attitude], so that you may prove [for yourselves] what is the good and acceptable and perfect will of God, even the thing which is good and acceptable and perfect [in His sight for you]."*

CONFORM

The Greek word for conformed is *suschématizó* which is derived from the root word *sysxēmatízō*. The word conveys assuming a similar outward form (expression) by following the same pattern or mold.[2] The New Oxford American Dictionary defines conform as to *"comply with rules, standards or laws; behave according to socially acceptable conventions or standards; be similar in form or type; agree."*[3]

We are not to pattern our behavior according to socially acceptable standards, rather we are instructed to renew our minds with the Word of God and allow the power of God to transform us so we are conformed to His image. We are called to operate according to the laws of the Kingdom of God, not of the world.

Unfortunately in our modern culture, the line between believers and unbelievers is blurred. As Christians we must ask ourselves some tough questions. If someone were to secretly follow us around recording our every word and action would the evidence support our claim that we are Christians? Or would they see us speaking and behaving in the same manner as unbelievers not being able to distinguish us as followers of Christ? Or even worse, would they label us as one of those Christian hypocrites who preach one standard, yet do not practice what they preach?

We may go through all of the Christian motions - pray, go to church, quote scripture, display our Christian symbols, but these activities do not mean we have a renewed mind. We can do all of these things and yet still be conformed to the world. In order to be transformed, we must begin to believe the Word of God, by getting it planted and rooted in our heart and get a revelation of our identity in Christ. We are called to be His ambassadors here on earth representing Him and the only way to do that is to get to know Him through His Word.[4]

TRANSFORM

The word transformed in this verse comes from the Greek word *metamorphoō* which means to change into another form.[5] *Vine's Concise Dictionary of the Bible* offers the following definition: *to change into another form, "be transformed", the obligation being to undergo a complete change which, under the power of God, will find expression in character and conduct.*[6]

So how can we tell if someone has a renewed mind? Evidence of transformation will be demonstrated by godly character and conduct. Godly character and conduct will become "second nature" as we allow the Holy Spirit to flow from our spirit, into our soul and into our body.

RENEW

The word renew, *anakainoó,* in this verse means to be changed into a new kind of life as opposed to the former corrupt state.[7] *Vine's Concise Dictionary of the Bible* states *"to make new - the adjustment of the moral and spiritual vision and thinking to the mind of God, which is designed to have a transforming effect upon the life."* It also goes on to say the action described in Romans 12:2 involves a willing response on the part of the believer.[8] Renewing the mind is an act of your will.

It does not automatically happen. It is how we become sanctified. We must renew our minds to be able to present ourselves holy to God and to know the will of God and walk in it. By renewing our minds we are transformed into the image of Christ.

Simply put, to renew your mind means to renovate your mind. Picture an old run down house that has been purchased by a new owner and will undergo extensive renovations. Many times renovation involves completely gutting the inside of the house. The basic structure or framework of the house is left intact, although the inside is completely emptied of its contents. After the structure is completely renovated it has both a beautiful exterior and interior. All of the contents of the interior are sparkling and new. The home might be filled with a crystal chandelier, beautiful works of art, new furniture, etc. But what if the new owner only dresses up the outside and doesn't do any work on the inside? Does it serve any purpose to fix and maintain the outside of the house when the inside is full of junk and decay? There isn't any value in that. It is the same with us when we are saved.

Jesus has purchased us and it is His desire to renovate us from the inside out. After we are saved, we must begin the process of purging our inner man of all of the old ways of thinking and behaving and allow the Holy Spirit do a beautiful work in us. Too many Christians neglect the interior. We spend time and money making the exterior look pleasing to others and to ourselves, but we fail to make the necessary changes deep within our soul. We may look great on the outside, but on the inside we are a mess. The old run down house that is filled with junk represents a mind that is not renewed and must be renovated.

Exchanging Our Thoughts for God's Thoughts

We have been taught to renew our minds by reading the Word of God. However, merely knowing what the Word of God says does not always produce the desired results in our lives. We may believe the Word of God is true when we read it or hear it, but for some reason it just doesn't seem to be producing fruit in our lives. I suspect many reading this book have had the following thoughts: *Why isn't the Word of God working for me in my life? I read the Word and I confess the Word, but I still don't see any change. What is wrong with me? Maybe I don't have enough faith.* When we don't see any results in our lives we become discouraged and begin to come up with a list of reasons why the Word isn't working, some of which might be:

- God is willing to do these things for others, but he won't do them for me.
- God must be mad at me.
- I must not be good enough to receive anything from God.
- I must be doing something wrong.

Perhaps one of the greatest tragedies is we get to a point where we wrongly interpret the Word of God to find an explanation for our circumstances. It is important not to take Scripture out of context and we must consider the content of the Bible in its entirety. We are not to read the Word of God through our eyes with our own understanding, but through His eyes with the understanding of the Holy Spirit. We may think what we believe about God and His Word is true, but in fact it may not be true.

Have you ever noticed many people who are poor claim it is godly to be poor and they condemn those who are wealthy? After all, money is the root of all evil they say, or it's easier for a camel to pass through the eye of a needle than for a rich man to enter heaven. These statements demonstrate a false humility that serves to make them feel better about their situation and reinforces their acceptance of their belief. They have convinced themselves they are more spiritual and they ignore the hundreds of other scriptures concerning prosperity and only focus on those that support their point of view. The Bible says the *love* of money is the root of all evil, not money is the root of all evil. Money is simply a tool that can be used for evil purposes or godly purposes. If you have just enough to get by, then you do not have the ability to be a blessing to others. Poverty is not the will of God. It is a mindset, usually passed down from generation to generation.

Often the same issue is seen with those who are suffering with sickness and disease. Many people think, *God is teaching me a lesson* or *I am suffering for the Lord.* Nonsense. God does not get any glory when a child of His is sick, nor does He get any glory when a child of His is living in poverty. We share in his sufferings, means we suffer for the sake of the gospel just as Jesus did when he endured persecution, not that we suffer in sickness or poverty.

Was Jesus sick when he walked this earth? No. Is Jesus sick now? No. As He is so are we in this world.[9] If Jesus died on the cross taking our sickness and disease,[10] and He has no sickness and we are in Him, how is it God's will for any of us to be sick? There are many reasons why someone has sickness or disease, but one of them certainly isn't because it's God's will or because He is teaching them a lesson. It could be because of poor choices – not doing what we know to do to take care of our bodies such as eating properly, exercising, or sleeping. Sometimes our disobedience opens up the door to the enemy to wreak havoc in our lives. Sickness can come for any number of reasons.

Jesus came so we could have an abundant life.[11] Being poor and sick is not living in abundance. God is glorified when His children are prospering in every way. God has already prepared for us everything we need. We simply need to take a hold of it and walk right into it.

Jesus Himself said a house divided against itself cannot stand.[12] God does not bring sickness. If God were to bring sickness and disease upon people, then He would be operating in contradiction to His nature. Sickness and disease come from the curse. If we are suffering from disease, poverty, etc. somehow the door has been opened. It is up to us to find the open door and slam it shut once and for all and we must be diligent to not open any other points of access. In this book we will explore "open doors" that keep us from receiving according to the Word of God.

I believe much of the reason why we are unable to receive all God has for us is because we have so many wrong beliefs as well as unbelief planted in our hearts. These beliefs may be developed through our life experiences or faulty teaching. As Christians we possess many erroneous beliefs and do not realize it. We are filled with either misinformation or unbelief or both. To put it bluntly, we are walking around believing a bunch of lies – lies about ourselves, lies about others and lies about God. We have been deceived into accepting lies as truth.

Think About What You Are Thinking About

Everything starts with a thought. Everything. There is nothing that exists today that was not first conceived from a thought. Our thoughts precede our words, our words precede our actions. Words are vehicles to express thoughts. All of our words and actions have their origin in a thought and we are a product of our thoughts. Joyce Meyer always says *"Where the mind goes, the man follows."* We encounter problems when we allow the wrong thoughts to take root. Once a thought takes root, it becomes a belief. The only way to remove a wrong belief is to identify and destroy the root and then replace it with the truth of God's Word.

So why might God's Word not be working? My own journey revealed to me one important step that too often is missed. We do not consider that we have wrong beliefs planted in our subconscious mind that are in conflict with the Word of God and prevent us from being able to receive the Word of God. To produce the desired harvest we must be successful in renewing the mind. First we must work to identify wrong beliefs, then uproot them and plant the truth of the Word of God in their place. In renewing our mind an exchange must take place – we must exchange our thoughts and ideas for God's thoughts and ideas. One way we do this is by meditating on the Word of God which helps us to take our thoughts captive.

Ralph Waldo Emerson said "*Life consists of what a man is thinking about all day.*" We will always move in the direction of our most dominant thoughts whether we realize it or not. What do you spend most of your time thinking about? Proverbs 23:7 tells us *"as a man thinks in his heart so is he."* The Hebrew word for heart is *nephesh* which means "soul" and in some instances may refer to the unconscious, or what we would call the subconscious mind.[13]

> [7] *For as he thinks in his heart, so is he. As one who reckons, he says to you, eat and drink, yet his heart is not with you [but is grudging the cost].* ~ **Proverbs 23:7 AMP**

What does this tell us? It is easy for someone to "talk the talk", although they may believe the exact opposite. How many of us go through the motions of saying and doing what we think we are supposed to say and do in front of others, yet speak and act differently behind closed doors? I think many Christians are quite skilled at "talking the talk", but often lack authenticity. I am not suggesting they are intentionally being deceptive, rather I think many are afraid of what others might think of them if they were to be honest about their struggles. Often times our words say one thing, but our actions that come from our beliefs are contradictory. We must expose the lies we believe and exchange them for truth to live an authentic life in Christ.

Uprooting Wrong Beliefs

We must allow the Word of God to take root in our hearts and allow it to change our perception of ourselves, others and God. The Bible must become more than just words on a page that we read and mentally agree with – it must become planted and rooted in our heart. As Christians we say we believe the Bible, but do we really believe what is in the Word of God? We are called believers, but do we really believe?

I spent most of my life claiming the Word of God to be true, but I was not seeing the desired results in my life. Why? It was a lack of application. But why the lack of application? On my journey of inner healing I came to the realization I had hidden unbelief. If I truly believed the Word applied to me and if I believed it would work for me I would act on it. So the question was why did I believe it wouldn't work? Did I think God was a liar? No, of course not! Rather I had trouble believing He would do what He said He would do for me.

I found myself coming up with lists of reasons why God could not or would not do certain things for me. Those reasons consisted of things I was doing I should not have been doing and things I should have been doing I was not doing. This is referred to as performance orientation. One of my stumbling blocks was a belief I must perform in a perfect manner to receive from God. I believed the Word to be true, but it was a faulty perception of who God is and who I am that stood in the way of receiving all God has for me.

If you grew up being taught under the word of faith movement you are familiar with the phrase "confession brings possession", and while that is a true statement, it is an oversimplification of how we go about appropriating the promises of God. Yes, confessing the Word of God helps to plant that seed in our heart and in some cases we see the fruit of our confession, but what about those cases for which we do not? How many of us have applied this principle of confession only to keep getting the same thing we have always been getting?

> *8"For my thoughts are not your thoughts, neither are your ways my ways," declares the LORD. 9"As the heavens are higher than the earth, so are my ways higher than your ways and my thoughts than your thoughts. 10As the rain and the snow come down from heaven, and do not return to it without watering the earth and making it bud and flourish, so that it yields seed for the sower and bread for the eater, 11so is my word that goes out from my mouth: It will not return to me empty, but will accomplish what I desire and achieve the purpose for which I sent it.*
> **~ Isaiah 55:8-11 AMP**

God's Word is purposed to always bring a harvest. The Word of God is incorruptible seed that will produce after itself, so why is the incorruptible seed not producing?[14] I can confess a scripture 100 times per day for an entire year yet still see no results. Why would a seed that contains a guaranteed harvest not produce? The only reason is because it is not planted and cultivated properly.

> *3Give attention to this! Behold, a sower went out to*
> *sow. 4And as he was sowing, some seed fell along the path, and the birds came and ate it up.5Other seed [of the same kind] fell on ground full of rocks, where it had not much soil; and at once it sprang up, because it had no depth of*
> *soil; 6And when the sun came up, it was scorched, and*
> *because it had not taken root, it withered away. 7Other seed [of the same kind] fell among thorn plants, and the thistles grew and pressed together and utterly choked*
> *and suffocated it, and it yielded no grain.* ***8And other seed [of the same kind] fell into good (well-adapted) soil and brought forth grain, growing up and increasing, and yielded up to thirty times as much, and sixty times as much, and even a hundred times as much as had been sown.*** **~ Mark 4:3-8 AMP**

> *13And He said to them, Do you not discern and understand this parable? How then is it possible for you to discern*
> *and understand all the parables? 14The sower sows the*
> *Word. 15The ones along the path are those who have the Word sown [in their hearts], but when they hear, Satan comes at once and [by force] takes away the message*
> *which is sown in them. 16And in the same way the ones sown upon stony ground are those who, when they hear the Word, at once receive and accept and welcome it with*
> *joy; 17And they have no real root in themselves, and so they endure for a little while; then when trouble or persecution arises on account of the Word, they are immediately offended (become displeased, indignant,*
> *resentful) and they stumble and fall away. 18And the ones sown among the thorns are others who hear the*
> *Word; 19Then the cares and anxieties of the world and*

> *distractions of the age, and the pleasure and delight and false glamour and deceitfulness of riches, and the craving and passionate desire for other things creep in and choke and suffocate the Word, and it becomes fruitless.* [20]***And those sown on the good (well-adapted) soil are the ones who hear the Word and receive and accept and welcome it and bear fruit--some thirty times as much as was sown, some sixty times as much, and some [even] a hundred times as much.*** **~ Mark 4:13-20 AMP**

Three of the four types of ground were unproductive. In this parable, the problem wasn't with the seed because the seed was of the same kind. The seed wasn't any different. It was the environment in which it was placed that determined the harvest. If we are not reaping a harvest, then we first must determine if the Word is being planted properly. The same Word has been given to all of us. Since we all have the same seed, it will produce its intended result for each of us.

We miss out on our harvest because of our unbelief and our wrong beliefs. Mentally agreeing the Word of God is true does not bring the harvest, rather receiving it into our heart and cultivating it produces a harvest. True belief comes from the heart, not the mind. When we hear or study the Word, it must pass through our mind to get planted in our heart. Simply knowing what the Word of God says isn't enough; we must believe it and accept it as truth. In order to believe and receive, we must identify any hidden inner beliefs that are in conflict with God's Word.

> [8]*But what does it say? The Word (God's message in Christ) is near you,* ***on your lips and in your heart****; that is, the Word (the message, the basis and object) of faith which we preach,* [9]*But what does it say? The Word (God's message in Christ) is near you,* ***on your lips and in your heart;*** *that is, the Word Because if you acknowledge and confess with your lips that Jesus is Lord and* ***in your heart believe*** *(adhere to, trust in, and rely on the truth)*

> *that God raised Him from the dead, you will be saved.* [10]***For with the heart a person believes*** *(adheres to, trusts in, and relies on Christ) and so is justified (declared righteous, acceptable to God),* ***and with the mouth he confesses*** *(declares openly and speaks out freely his faith)* ***and confirms [his] salvation.*** **~ Romans 10:8-10 AMP**

Isn't it interesting this verse says we *believe with our heart* and confess with our mouth? It doesn't say we believe with our mind or as a result of confessing with our mouths. *Our confession is evidence of our inward belief.* Belief is conceived in the heart and the words of the mouth confirm salvation.

The most important belief we will ever hold is that of accepting Jesus Christ as our Lord and Savior. If receiving salvation is contingent upon believing in our heart, not merely confessing the Word, why wouldn't receiving all of the other promises of God hinge on the same condition? It is possible to confess Jesus Christ as Lord and Savior with your mouth, yet not truly believe it in your heart.

Luke's account of the Sower and the Seed provides some additional insight not evident in Mark's version:

> [5]*A sower went out to sow seed; and as he sowed, some fell along the traveled path and was trodden underfoot, and the birds of the air ate it up.* [6]*And some [seed] fell on the rock, and as soon as it sprouted, it withered away because it had no moisture.* [7]*And other [seed] fell in the midst of the thorns, and the thorns grew up with it and choked it [off].* [8]*And some seed fell into good soil, and grew up and yielded a crop a hundred times [as great].* **~ Luke 8:5-8 AMP**

> [11]*Now the meaning of the parable is this: The seed is the Word of God.* [12]*Those along the traveled road are the people who have heard; then the devil comes and carries away the message out of their hearts, that they may not*

> *believe acknowledge Me as their Savior and devote*
> *themselves to Me) and be saved [here and hereafter].*
> *13And those upon the rock [are the people] who, when*
> *they hear [the Word], receive and welcome it with joy;*
> *but these have no root. They believe for a while, and in*
> *time of trial and temptation fall away (withdraw and*
> *stand aloof). 14And as for what fell among the thorns,*
> *these are [the people] who hear, but as they go on their*
> *way they are choked and suffocated with the anxieties*
> *and cares and riches and pleasures of life, and their fruit*
> *does not ripen (come to maturity and perfection). 15But as*
> *for that [seed] in the good soil, these are [the people] who,*
> *hearing the Word, hold it fast in a just (noble, virtuous)*
> *and worthy heart, and steadily bring forth fruit with*
> *patience.* ~ **Luke 8:11-15 AMP**

The different types of ground in the parable of the Sower and the Seed can be used to describe the various conditions of our soul.

Seed along the path. The seed was not able to be planted in any soil therefore it was unable to produce. It was "trodden under foot." This is the Word that is preached, but discarded by the intended receiver. Often this happens with the message of salvation, but it applies to the truths in God's Word we choose not to receive after we are saved. If we do not receive the seed and plant it properly, it will not produce. It is important to weed out all of the beliefs we have that are contrary to the Word of God, so we are not unknowingly discarding His Word. The most common problem we have is we may believe the Word of God is true, but for various reasons we may not believe it is true for us. Satan wants to convince us God will not do for us what His Word promises. We cannot accept the truth if we believe a lie. Someone who believes it is godly to be poor is unable to receive the seed of prosperity; therefore they will remain in poverty. Likewise, someone who believes it is God's will for them to be sick, will not be able to receive the seed of healing and they will remain sick.

Seed among the rocks. The seed fell among rock where there was little soil. As soon as it sprouted, it withered because it did not have deep roots. This describes those who hear the word of God and get excited about it and mentally agree with it, but have not fully received it into their heart. Eventually they withdraw from God and abandon His Word when they do not see immediate results or encounter any resistance.

Seed among the thorns. The seed that fell among thorns, had enough soil to produce, but the thorns and thistles prevented full maturation. The thorns and thistles must be cleared out to allow the Word to come into full maturation. The Word has been planted in their heart, but they do not reach spiritual maturity because they get caught up in the distractions of life. This would represent what we refer to as the carnal Christian - one controlled by fleshly desires and not controlled by the Spirit. Issues within our soul will keep the Word from producing.

Seed planted in good soil. The seed planted in the good soil represents those who hear the Word and guard it and bring forth fruit. This soil was properly cultivated. There were no thistles or thorns; there were no rocks, just fertile soil. The soil had been purged and it was well adapted, therefore the seed was able to produce a full harvest. We must purge ourselves of anything that prevents us from fully receiving God's Word.

In Mark 11:23-24 AMP Jesus said:

> *"Truly I tell you, whoever says to this mountain, Be lifted up and thrown into the sea! and* ***does not doubt at all in his heart but believes that what he says will take place****, it will be done for him. For this reason I am telling you, whatever you ask for in prayer,* ***believe (trust and be confident) that it is granted to you, and you will [get it].***

Once again we see true belief comes from the heart, *kardia* which refers to the mind, character, inner self, will, or intention.[15] Belief must reside in our soul. Jesus said we must believe to be able to receive.

Examining the Heart Condition

> [12]*For the Word that God speaks is alive and full of power [making it active, operative, energizing, and effective]; it is sharper than any two-edged sword, penetrating to the dividing line of the breath of life (soul) and [the immortal] spirit, and of joints and marrow [of the deepest parts of our nature], exposing and sifting and analyzing and judging the very thoughts and purposes of the heart.*
> **~ Hebrews 4:12 AMP**

Chapter 1 discussed the difference between body, soul and spirit. You are a spirit being who possesses a soul and lives in a physical body. The Word of God helps us to determine the condition of our soul, or what we are thinking in our "heart", and whether or not our soul is in agreement with the Holy Spirit that resides in our regenerated spirit. The Word of God tries and tests our motives.

The Greek word for "two-edged" is *dístomos* when used figuratively means *"what penetrates at every point of contact, coming in or going out."* [16] The Word assists us in differentiating between what is of our soul and what is of the Holy Spirit. When we drink in the Word it penetrates deep within us. When we speak out the Word, it penetrates deep within us. We must allow the word to permeate our soul and root out those areas of unbelief and disobedience. We must feed on it continually until we believe it whole heartedly - not just agreeing with it intellectually, but knowing deep within it is true and it is true for us.

When we study and meditate on the Word of God our minds become renewed to His ways. Our renewed spirit bears witness with the truth as we read the Word or as God speaks directly to us. The study of God's Word helps our soul – mind, will, and emotions – come into agreement with our regenerated spirit man. The Word examines our innermost thoughts - those unspoken things that often go unnoticed, but the Sword cuts deep to expose those things so we might be transformed. The Word of God is the Sword of the Spirit and it is the most powerful offensive weapon we have.[17] One way to prepare for any battle is by meditating on the Word of God.

Meditating on the Word of God

> [8] *This Book of the Law shall not depart out of your mouth, but you shall meditate on it day and night, that you may observe and do according to all that is written in it. For then you shall make your way prosperous, and then you shall deal wisely and have good success.* ~ **Joshua 1:8 AMP**

To meditate means to murmur or to ponder.[18] Meditating involves not only thinking on God's Word, but speaking God's Word as well. We can't live in accordance with God's Word unless we know what it says. We must take the time to become intimately familiar with it. Meditation is the vehicle that allows us to exchange our thoughts for God's thoughts. When we study and meditate on the Word of God our minds become renewed to His ways.

To commit something to memory, you say it over and over again. Eventually you don't even need to think about the words, they just flow naturally. When we are in the process of renewing our minds our goal should be the same - to become so full of God's Word that we are speaking it out and acting on it without having to think about it. It should just naturally flow through our words and our behavior.

Renewing the mind is not a one-time event. It involves dedicating ourselves to the study of God's Word and meditating on it habitually. We must practice it daily so we will be ready to bring forth fruit when it is the appointed season. The Word sustains us and waters our soul.

> *Blessed (happy, fortunate, prosperous, and enviable) is the man who walks and lives not in the counsel of the ungodly [following their advice, their plans and*

> *purposes], nor stands [submissive and inactive] in the path where sinners walk, nor sits down [to relax and rest] where the scornful [and the mockers] gather.* [2] ***But his delight and desire are in the law of the Lord, and on His law (the precepts, the instructions, the teachings of God) he habitually meditates (ponders and studies) by day and by night.*** [3] ***And he shall be like a tree firmly planted [and tended] by the streams of water, ready to bring forth its fruit in its season; its leaf also shall not fade or wither; and everything he does shall prosper [and come to maturity].*** **~ Psalm 1:1-3 AMP**

Trees get nourishment and drink in water from the roots. As long as there is a continual supply of nutrients and water, a tree will flourish. The same is true of our soul. When we are rooted in God and we drink in the water of His Word each day we will bring forth fruit and prosper in all God has purposed for us to do. As we meditate on the Word of God, we will be firmly planted and rooted, not fading or withering like the seed that fell on the path, the seed that fell on the stone or the seed that was choked by thorns and thistles.

God's Word is full of wisdom which will lead us to success when we give attention to it and apply it on a daily basis. When the Word of God is rooted at the center of our heart, we will have success in every area of our lives. It doesn't mean we won't have any trouble, but we will flourish in spite of it. When we delight ourselves in the Lord, He will give us the desires of our heart.[19] As we draw close to Him, His desires become our desires. Everything we do will prosper when it is done in accordance with the will of God.

> [20] *My son, attend to my words; consent and submit to my sayings.* [21] *Let them not depart from your sight; keep them in the center of your heart.* [22] *For they are life to those who find them, healing and health to all their flesh.* [23] *Keep and guard your heart with all vigilance and above all that you guard, for out of it flow the springs of life.*

~ Proverbs 4:20-23 AMP

The Hebrew word for heart used in Proverbs 4:21-23 is *leb*, which refers to the inner man, his mind and will.[20] God's Word must be firmly planted in our soul so it rules our mind, will and emotions. Proverbs 4 tells us attending to God's Word, or meditating on it, brings healing and health. As the Word of God takes root in our soul, we can expect His life to flow from His spirit into our spirit, into our soul and into our body, however we must be on guard regarding what we allow to flow into our soul and be vigilant about taking thoughts captive.

Taking Thoughts Captive

We must use caution concerning thoughts and images we allow to take up residence in our mind. Although at times it might be challenging, it is possible to exercise control over our thoughts.

> 3*For though we walk (live) in the flesh, we are not carrying on our warfare according to the flesh and using mere human weapons.* 4*For the weapons of our warfare are not physical [weapons of flesh and blood], but they are mighty before God for the overthrow and destruction of strongholds,* 5*[Inasmuch as we] refute arguments and theories and reasonings and every proud and lofty thing that sets itself up against the [true] knowledge of God; and we lead every thought and purpose away captive into the obedience of Christ (the Messiah, the Anointed One),*
> 6*Being in readiness to punish every [insubordinate for his] disobedience, when your own submission and obedience [as a church] are fully secured and complete.*
> **~ 2 Corinthians 10:3-6 AMP**

What does it mean to lead our thoughts and purposes captive to the obedience of Christ? It means we must test our thoughts as to whether or not they line up with the Word of God and if they do not, we need to counter the contradiction to God's Word by renouncing and refusing to accept the contrary thought. We must then speak out the Word of God concerning that particular subject. For example, when the thought comes to your mind that says you are unworthy of love you must reject that thought and replace it with the truth of God's Word which says you are worthy and you are loved by God unconditionally. By taking our thoughts captive to the obedience of Christ, strongholds cannot be established. The only way we can be successful in taking thoughts captive is to know what the Word of God says and to renew our minds with His truth. In Luke 4, Jesus shows us how to respond to those suggestions:

> *Then Jesus,* ***full of and controlled by the Holy Spirit,***
> *returned from the Jordan and was led in [by] the [Holy]*
> *Spirit 2 For (during) forty days in the wilderness (desert),*
> *where He was tempted (tried, tested exceedingly) by the*
> *devil. And He ate nothing during those days, and when*
> *they were completed, He was hungry. 3Then the devil said*
> *to Him, If You are the Son of God, order this stone to turn*
> *into a loaf [of bread].* ***4And Jesus replied to him, It is***
> ***written,*** *Man shall not live and be sustained by (on)*
> *bread alone but by every word and expression of God.*
> *5Then the devil took Him up to a high mountain and*
> *showed Him all the kingdoms of the habitable world in a*
> *moment of time [in the twinkling of an eye]. 6 And he said*
> *to Him, To You I will give all this power and authority and*
> *their glory (all their magnificence, excellence,*
> *preeminence, dignity, and grace), for it has been turned*
> *over to me, and I give it to whomever I will. 7 Therefore if*
> *You will do homage to and worship me [just once], it shall*
> *all be Yours.* ***8And Jesus replied to him, Get behind Me,***
> ***Satan! It is written,*** *You shall do homage to and worship*
> *the Lord your God, and Him only shall you serve. 9 Then he*
> *took Him to Jerusalem and set Him on a gable of the*
> *temple, and said to Him, If You are the Son of God, cast*
> *Yourself down from here; 10For it is written, He will*
> *give His angels charge over you to guard and watch over*
> *you closely and carefully; 11And on their hands they will*

bear you up, lest you strike your foot against a stone.
[12]***And Jesus replied to him, [The Scripture] says,*** *You*
shall not tempt (try, test exceedingly) the Lord your God.
[13]*And when the devil had ended every [the complete cycle*
of] temptation, he [temporarily] left Him [that is, stood
off from Him] until another more opportune and
favorable time. **~ Luke 4:1-13 AMP**

What did Jesus do? He simply spoke the written Word. Jesus countered each temptation of the enemy by speaking out the written Word of God. After being rejected twice, Satan began to quote Scripture! He tried to tempt Jesus by taking the word out of context! Jesus plainly responded with the greater truth. After Jesus responded with the Word of God three times, the devil left him. It may take you speaking the Word of God out more than three times, but bless God if you keep speaking the Word to the enemy he will leave. When he returns, and he will, you must continue to believe the Word and do more of the same. The Sword of the Spirit will never fail when you use it in conjunction with a believing heart.

It is important to notice Jesus was not operating in His own strength, but He was fully controlled by the power of the Holy Spirit. Likewise, we must submit ourselves to the power of the Holy Spirit. We are able to become full of and controlled by the Holy Spirit when we get to know Him through His Word and through spending time with Him. A renewed mind is able to be controlled by the Spirit and provides the means for walking in the Spirit.

Walking in the Spirit

Therefore, [there is] now no condemnation (no adjudging guilty of wrong) for those who are in Christ Jesus, who live [and] walk not after the dictates of the flesh, but after the dictates of the Spirit.....[4]*So that the righteous and just requirement of the Law might be fully met in us who live and move not in the ways of the flesh but in the ways of the Spirit [our lives governed not by the standards and according to the dictates of the flesh, but controlled by the Holy Spirit]. [5]For those who are according to the flesh and are controlled by its unholy desires set their minds on and pursue those things which gratify the flesh, but those who are according to the Spirit and are controlled by the desires of the Spirit set their minds on and seek those things which gratify the [Holy] Spirit. [6]Now the mind of the flesh [which is sense and reason without the Holy Spirit] is death [death that comprises all the miseries arising from sin, both here and hereafter]. But the mind of the [Holy] Spirit is life and [soul] peace [both now and forever]. [7][That is] because the mind of the flesh [with its carnal thoughts and purposes] is hostile to God, for it does not submit itself to God's Law; indeed it cannot.* ~ **Romans 8:1, 4-7 AMP**

In the prior chapter of Romans, Paul described his internal battle, desiring to do what is right, but struggling to do so. In Romans 8, he offered some insight on how to overcome the battle within his soul.

The Greek word for flesh in Romans 8 is *sarka* which involves *"making decisions according to self; done apart from faith in God."* Making decisions according to the flesh, or according to self, results from the untouched parts of us not yet transformed by God.[21] The mind of the flesh is a mindset based solely on sense and reason and operates in contradiction to the Word of God, thus it leads to death, but the mind of the Spirit brings life and peace. It is our mindset that controls our actions. We must submit our mind to the Word of God. Whatever we yield our mind to and submit our mind to will ultimately control our actions.

If then you have been raised with Christ [to a new life, thus sharing His resurrection from the dead], aim at and seek the [rich, eternal treasures] that are above, where Christ is, seated at the right hand of God. [2]And set your minds and keep them set on what is above (the higher things), not on the things that are on the earth.

~ Colossians 3:1-2 AMP

We cannot expect to have godly actions if we do not think godly thoughts. We must make a choice to set our mind on the things of God and keep our mind set on things of God.

> [16]*But I say, walk and live [habitually] in the [Holy] Spirit [responsive to and controlled and guided by the Spirit]; then you will certainly not gratify the cravings and desires of the flesh (of human nature without God).* [17]*For the desires of the flesh are opposed to the [Holy] Spirit, and the [desires of the] Spirit are opposed to the flesh (godless human nature); for these are antagonistic to each other [continually withstanding and in conflict with each other], so that you are not free but are prevented from doing what you desire to do.* **~ Galatians 5:16-17 AMP**

Galatians 5:16 instructs us to "walk in the Spirit" and by doing so we will not fulfill the lusts of the flesh. So what does it mean to walk in the Spirit? It means we are led by the Spirit and living out the Word of God each and every day. How can we tell if we are walking in the Spirit? If we are walking in the Spirit we will demonstrate the fruits of the Spirit - love, joy, peace, patience, kindness, goodness, faithfulness, gentleness and self control. To walk in the Spirit we must renew our mind.

Evidence of a Renewed Mind

So how can you tell if your mind is renewed or if someone else has a renewed mind? Evidence of true transformation is demonstrated through godly character and conduct. Remember the examples of riding a bike and driving a car? Godly behaviors and actions will become second nature to us. We will automatically think and act like God. We must become so full of God's Word that no matter where we are, no matter what we are doing, no matter what happens we can automatically act in accordance with God's Word. We will no longer be a prisoner to "knee jerk" reactions, nor will we need to pause and think about what to say or do. God's Word planted in our heart and mind will flow from our lips and be manifested in our actions.

If the fruit of the spirit is not evident in our lives, then we have lots of work to do in the area of renewing the mind. The only way for us to walk in the Spirit is to renew our minds and submit ourselves to the Holy Spirit. We must be led by the Spirit to fulfill God's plan for our lives.

Do Not Faint!

> [3]*Just think of Him Who endured from sinners such grievous opposition and bitter hostility against Himself [reckon up and consider it all in comparison with your trials], so that you may not grow weary or exhausted, losing heart and relaxing and fainting in your minds.*
> **~ Hebrews 12:3 AMP**

Joyce Meyer wrote a best-selling book *Battlefield of the Mind* and the title speaks for itself. There is a war in our mind and if we faint in our minds we lose the battle. Our greatest weapon to win the battle, is our mighty Sword - the Word of God. We must read it, speak it and choose to believe it. We begin to faint in our minds when we allow negative thoughts to overtake us and fill us with fear and doubt. Fainting in our minds causes us to give up and resign ourselves to the fact things will not change no matter what we do. We gain inner strength by meditating on the Word and renewing our mind with the Word. A renewed mind does not faint.

The state of our mind determines the state of our lives. What we constantly meditate on eventually becomes our reality. If we are defeated in our minds we will live a defeated life. If we are victorious in our minds we will live a victorious life. We must remain vigilant in taking our thoughts captive to the obedience of Christ. Each day we must be determined to win the war in our minds by keeping our minds fixed on the Word of God. Today make the decision you will not faint in your mind. Use your mighty Sword to defeat the lies the enemy attempts to plant in your mind.

Chapter 4

Beliefs & Belief Systems

Have you ever asked yourself *"why do I behave the way I do?"* The simple answer to this question is our behavior is determined by our mindsets or our beliefs. We only act on and out of what we personally believe to be true.

Mindsets

So what is a mindset? What does it mean to "set our mind" on something? Here is one definition I believe sums up all of the definitions I found: *a fixed mental attitude or disposition that predetermines a person's responses to and interpretations of situations.*[1] So what exactly is a "fixed mental attitude"? The definition of fixed is *"fastened securely in position, predetermined or inflexibly held"*.[2] Does that sound like anyone you know? We all know people who have made up their mind regarding a particular issue and no matter what anyone says, even when they are presented with cold hard facts, they will not change their mind. Are you that person? If you answered yes, then you answered honestly, but if you answered no, let me ask this – is there something that you "know that you know" and you cannot be swayed from your position? We all feel that way about some things whether we are right or wrong. With that said mindsets can be either positive or negative. There is nothing wrong with having a mindset that affects your life and the lives of others around you in a positive way; but those negative mindsets will hinder a person in life and adversely affect the relationships they have. Sometimes if we are not careful the negative mindset of another person can begin to shape our mindsets and how we view ourselves.

One day as I was researching the topic of mindsets, I stumbled upon a study on mindsets, where a mindset was defined as "a particular point of view through which one experiences reality."[3] I believe this statement succinctly summarizes the above dictionary definition and takes it a step further – our mindsets affect our perception which is our reality. This explains why a group of 100 people sitting in a room listening to the same speaker can hear the same exact words, yet each may respond very differently to what has been said. Sometimes it seems almost impossible to believe that two people have listened to the same speaker since their reactions are polar opposites. The different reactions are due to their individual mindsets which have predetermined their responses to what was spoken.

Have you ever had a conversation with someone who suddenly became angry because of something you said? When you inquired about why they were angry what happened? Most likely they repeated back to you what they "heard" and you found yourself wondering how they made the leap from point A to point B, because what they "heard" is not what you said. You certainly didn't mean your words the way they were received. They reacted in anger because of their perception of what was said and their perception occurred due to their mindset. How many times have you been this person? Situations like these are all too common and most people just seem to accept that "John has always been that way and always will be" or "I have always been this way and always will be", when in fact both John and you can change your behavior and that change starts with altering your mindset.

So how does one go about changing their mindsets? A mindset is simply a habitual way of thinking, so to change our mindset we need to change our ways of thinking. So the next question to ask is what determines our thoughts? Our thoughts are determined by what we meditate on – we become what we think about – garbage in, garbage out. What are you listening to? What are you reading? What are you and your friends and family talking about? Changing your mindsets starts with choosing to meditate on what is positive rather than what is negative and permanently replacing negative thoughts with positive thoughts. As we learned in Chapter 3, this is accomplished by renewing or minds with the truth of God's Word.

How & When Mindsets are Developed

We often hear about the formative years in childhood and how crucial that time is in developing a person. It is believed most of our mindsets become rooted and established at a particularly young age. We may not be aware of those controlling our actions as adults. In extreme cases, a stronghold may be developed. We develop habits and patterns of behavior because of mindsets that come from our experiences and observations of our environment. As adults we wonder why we say what we say and do what we do. We think - *What is wrong with me? Why do I keep repeating the same patterns?* and the answers to these questions and others like them elude us.

Unfortunately children do not yet possess the cognitive abilities to fully evaluate a situation and develop a rational and informed position. Therefore children often make faulty judgments. As children, mindsets may be established as a result of traumatic events or may be established through observation and repetition. Too often the hurts, traumas and negative experiences of our childhood cause us to believe lies about ourselves, others and even God. If we perceive ourselves and/or others in a negative manner or have a false understanding of the nature of God, the quality of our lives is greatly diminished.

Beliefs

Sometimes the terms belief and mindset are used interchangeably, but it is actually our beliefs that form our mindsets.

The New Oxford American Dictionary defines a belief as *an acceptance that a statement is true or that something exists. Something one accepts as true or real; a firmly held opinion or conviction.*[4] Notice a belief is an *acceptance* of a statement or thing being true. Not every belief is based in truth. In fact, it is possible to believe something that is completely false.

The sum total of our beliefs form our belief system which drives our behavior. A belief system may also be referred to as a cognitive belief system, which is a system that *"provides a core set of values in which we base everything we say and do. It is a mental system consisting of interrelated items of assumptions, beliefs, ideas and knowledge that an individual holds about anything concrete (person, group, object, etc.) or abstract (thoughts, theory, information) etc. It comprises an individual's world view and determines how he abstracts, filters and structures information received from the world around."*[5] This explains why two people can view the exact same situation and have two very different perceptions of what happened. What we accept as true determines our mindsets and our mindsets determine our perception. Furthermore, our mindsets drive the decisions we make and actions we take.

Dr. Wayne Dyer says *"A belief system is nothing more than a thought you've thought over and over again."* Our thought patterns determine our mindsets. Each thought is a seed that gets planted and takes root as you continue to meditate on it. Unfortunately one bad seed planted in childhood through a trauma or other significant event can have life-long repercussions.

Most of our beliefs are established at a particularly young age, yet we may not realize those beliefs that have become rooted and established and are controlling our actions as adults. We develop habits and patterns of behavior because of beliefs that come from our life experiences and from observations of our environment. Most of our behavior patterns are driven by beliefs that were formed by experiences during our childhood.

Importance of Beliefs

The beliefs we hold are important because our beliefs will ultimately determine our destiny. Awhile back I came across the following quote:

> *"If you accept a belief you reap a thought. If you sow a thought you reap an attitude. If you sow an attitude you reap an action. If you sow an action you reap a habit. If you sow a habit you reap character. If you sow a character you reap a destiny." ~Anonymous*

I actually believe the thought comes first – we think it before we believe it. If you accept a thought you reap a belief. We all have a God given destiny to fulfill, yet so many people go through life miserable and empty and leave this earth never having fulfilled that destiny. Why? Because of wrong beliefs – lies we have accepted - about ourselves, others and God.

Our beliefs affect our mindsets, perceptions, decisions, actions and reactions. We only act on and out of what we personally believe to be true. Each and every day we observe wrong behaviors and actions from others and even from ourselves. How many of us wake up each morning and make a conscious decision to behave badly, immorally or illegally on purpose? The vast majority of us are not that calculating. Many times when we are exhibiting these types of behaviors, we may not understand why we are demonstrating them particularly when we do not want to display certain behaviors. Most of us desire to do well and be good, yet often we seem to fall short. There are also those who may acknowledge their actions are wrong, yet they always find justification for those actions. When we make a choice, we make the choice believing it is the right one. However, it may be a wrong choice that we have somehow justified in our mind. We may tell ourselves that we are "righting a wrong" or we are entitled to act a certain way. Regardless, we are always acting out of our beliefs.

Belief Expectation Cycle

Here is an illustration of what is called the Belief-Expectation Cycle.

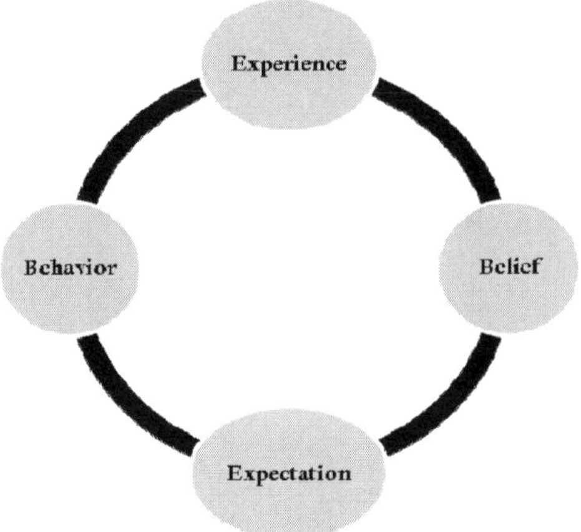

Source:
Restoring the Foundations:
An Integrated Approach to Healing Ministry

An EXPERIENCE causes us to form a BELIEF. Out of that belief we form an EXPECTATION. From that expectation then forms a BEHAVIOR. Our behavior influences the behavior of others which leads us back to a similar experience, which reinforces the belief and the cycle continues.[6] Our beliefs cause our expectations, the expectations shape our reality, and our reality influences our beliefs. To put it simply, our perception shapes our reality. We all have a unique filter through which we view the world around us and this filter is formed of all the beliefs we have developed through our life experiences.

The Belief-Expectation Cycle illustrates how we draw to ourselves what we expect. If we have experienced hurt from rejection, we may develop an expectation of rejection and each time we perceive someone is rejecting us, it reinforces the belief we will be rejected and that is what we continually come to expect. If we expect to be rejected we will experience just that – rejection - either perceived or real. When we expect people to reject us, rejection is all we are able to see. No matter what anyone says or does we will view their words and actions through the "filter" of rejection and even the slightest criticism or smallest suggestion will be perceived as rejection. Often we begin to act rejected before people have a chance to reject us and we behave in ways that eventually cause them to reject us. We end up getting more of what we don't want-rejection!

Our behavior affects both us and those around us and it creates a set up for our original type of experience to be repeated. Each time the cycle is completed, the belief is reinforced, because we continue to have the same experience. Unfortunately too often negative experiences, such as rejection, are driving this cycle. So how do we break this negative cycle? We break this negative cycle by identifying patterns of wrong thinking (lies) and replacing these patterns with right thinking (truth). This is accomplished by renewing our minds with God's Word.

> *"Do not be conformed to this world (this age), [fashioned after and adapted to its external, superficial customs], but be transformed (changed) by the [entire] renewal of your mind [by its new ideals and its new attitude], so that you may prove [for yourselves] what is the good and acceptable and perfect will of God, even the thing which is good and acceptable and perfect [in His sight for you]."*
> **~ Romans 12:2 AMP**

When you renew your mind to the truth of God's Word and you begin to see yourself the way God sees you, only then will you be transformed and able to fulfill your God given destiny and live the abundant life promised by God.

The Elephant in the Room

Adult elephants in captivity suffer from what has been termed by some as "baby elephant syndrome." Training of a baby elephant involves placing a chain around his ankle and tying the other end around a tree or to a large metal stake in the ground. When the baby elephant tries to wander off it is held back by the chain. If the elephant struggles to break free, the chain cuts deep into his flesh causing a painful wound. Eventually the baby elephant gives up as it realizes that its efforts are futile and the pain becomes too much to bear.

When an elephant reaches adulthood, because of its past experience, a 10,000 pound elephant can be held with the same chain tied to only a small wooden stake in the ground. Although the elephant now has the power to break free, it does not attempt to do so. It is held captive by its past experience. The elephant accepts its limitations and does not want to experience pain.

Akin to the baby elephant, some of our earliest experiences keep us shackled to our past rendering us unable to step into all God has prepared for us. When we are saved, we have the desire to run the race before us, but the chains of our past experiences too often are holding us captive. Years of painful experiences and memories cause us to shrink back and withdraw. We come to accept our limitations and we allow the pain of our past to hold us back. At times, even the mere thought of taking a step forward may cause us to wince in pain as the wounds from our past experiences are still fresh in our mind. Anticipating the sharp pain that may come, we resign ourselves to our present circumstances. We play it safe because we don't want to feel pain and we certainly don't want to risk getting wounded again. Additionally, our hurts and traumas shape our behaviors and responses toward others.

Too often the pain of our past becomes the "elephant in the room." Evidence of the pain exists in our lives, yet we refuse to talk about it and others may tip toe around us because we are too sensitive. When we choose to ignore and suppress our pain, it wreaks havoc in our lives, particularly in our relationships. When we make this choice, we are never able to step into God's best for our lives.

Unfortunately too many Christians carry a false belief that after they say the sinners prayer there is nothing else left to do, except sit back and wait on a miracle from God. Surrendering our lives to Christ does not mean everything will magically fall into place. It is up to us to appropriate all of God's promises. We must cooperate with Him by renewing our mind and being obedient to His leading. Like the man at the pool of Bethesda we must take action. We must get up and walk out our salvation. Jesus did not pick him up and throw him into the pool, He commanded the man to get up and walk and go about living in freedom. We have a part to play in becoming whole whether we like it or not. If we choose to live in denial, we will remain stuck. We must choose honesty and transparency while inviting Jesus into our pain so we can be healed once and for all.

At the time of salvation, our chains are broken by the power of the blood of Jesus, yet we continue to behave in a manner that is inconsistent with that truth. Too many Christians do not have revelation of who they are in Christ and remain bound by their chains through self imposed limitations. When a person has been in bondage for most of their life, he or she may not be able to recognize or comprehend their new found freedom and how to step into it. Similar to the fully mature elephant, we have the power to run free at any time because we possess the greatest power of all through the Holy Spirit that lives on the inside of us.

> [20] *Now to Him Who, by (in consequence of) the [action of His] power that is at work within us, is able to [carry out His purpose and] do superabundantly, far over and above all that we [dare] ask or think [infinitely beyond our highest prayers, desires, thoughts, hopes, or dreams]—*
> [21] *To Him be glory in the church and in Christ Jesus throughout all generations forever and ever. Amen (so be it).* ~ **Ephesians 3:20-21 AMP**

> [4] *Little children, you are of God [you belong to Him] and have [already] defeated and overcome them [the agents of the antichrist], because He Who lives in you is greater (mightier) than he who is in the world.* ~ **I John 4:4 AMP**

> [11]*And if the Spirit of Him Who raised up Jesus from the dead dwells in you, [then] He Who raised up Christ Jesus from the dead will also restore to life your mortal (short-lived, perishable) bodies through His Spirit Who dwells in you.* ~ **Romans 8:11 AMP**

> [16]*But whenever a person turns [in repentance] to the Lord, the veil is stripped off and taken away.* [17] *Now the Lord is the Spirit, and where the Spirit of the Lord is, there is liberty (emancipation from bondage, freedom).*[18] *And all of us, as with unveiled face, [because we] continued to behold [in the Word of God] as in a mirror the glory of the Lord, are constantly being transfigured into His very own image in ever increasing splendor and from one degree of glory to another; [for this comes] from the Lord [Who is] the Spirit.* ~ **2 Corinthians 3:16-18 AMP**

Jesus came to heal the broken hearted and set captives free! It is up to you to make the choice to break free once and for all. You do not need to remain in bondage to your past any longer.

> *"The Spirit of the LORD is upon Me, Because He has anointed Me To preach the gospel to the poor; He has sent Me to heal the brokenhearted, To proclaim liberty to the captives And recovery of sight to the blind, To set at liberty those who are oppressed;* ~ **Luke 4:18 NKJV**

God has provided us a way out. We do not need to stay stuck. As we surrender our pain to Him and fully embrace our identity in Christ we are finally able to break free, demonstrating the glory of God. It is a testament to His grace, mercy and His love.

Our Internal "Programs"

Often our "chains" exist in the form of hidden inner beliefs. In his book *If How To's Were Enough We Would All Be Skinny, Rich and Happy*, Brian Klemmer states:

> "People behave according to fundamental beliefs or subconscious thinking. You do not make 99 percent of your decisions; your programs make them for you, even though you think you are choosing. Your subconscious, or belief system, makes the majority of your decisions."[7]

Our behavior is an outward manifestation of what resides within our inner man. Negative behavior patterns are an outward reflection of an inner conflict, something that may be buried deep within our subconscious. Our subconscious "programs" direct our behavior on a daily basis. These programs are comprised of our belief systems.

So what triggers someone to change their behavior? Why do so many people continue on a path filled with destructive choices and behaviors? Brian Klemmer said *"No one changes their way of being until they see the high cost or price of their behavior."*[8] Most people do not fully understand the full ramifications of their behavior as it affects themselves and others. Change will not occur until they are able to see the cost of their behavior and are able to identify the underlying cause of the behavior. Simply treating "symptoms" and trying to change a behavior without fixing the underlying cause will not work. It is the same as when a medical doctor treats symptoms, but does not find the underlying cause for a patient's physical symptoms.

In his book, Klemmer uses a story about a sand wasp to illustrate how our subconscious programs guide our behavior. When a sand wasp brings food to its burrow, the sand wasp leaves its food at the opening of its burrow while it goes inside the burrow to search for any danger. The sand wasp returns for the food and brings it inside and then eats. In the illustration, Klemmer adds a hidden scientist who is watching the sand wasp from a distance. When the sand wasp leaves the food at the entrance of the burrow to go inside and inspect it, the scientist moves the food a few feet away from the burrow and then hides again. The sand wasp comes out of the burrow, discovers the food has been moved and moves it back to the edge of the burrow according to its instinct. It then goes back down into the hole to search for any danger. The scientist moves the food away from the burrow once again and the sand wasp returns and moves the food to the edge of the burrow and then goes back inside to look for any danger. This pattern will continue because the sand wasp is programmed to behave in this manner. As a result, the sand wasp dies from starvation. The sand wasp falls victim to its own programming.[9] This might seem like a silly illustration, but unfortunately many of us follow this same pattern in our lives. We keep repeating the same patterns of behavior over and over again, never getting the desired result and eventually we faint.

Perception vs. Reality

I believe many of our conflicts with others are due to a faulty perception. This is due to the fact that our beliefs form our perception and we all possess different belief systems. Perception is *"the process by which people translate sensory impressions into a coherent and unified view of the world around them. Though necessarily based on incomplete and unverified (unreliable) information, perception is equated with reality for most practical purposes and guides human behavior in general."*[10]

Your perception - your beliefs - determine your reality, which in turn determines your behavior. How we perceive the world around us is directly related to our established beliefs. Perception does not necessarily reflect what is happening, but rather how we think we are seeing what is happening. Our perception of a particular person or a situation may not be based in truth; in fact it may be completely false. Our perception is simply a point of view. Two people can view the same situation very differently and the perception of each is their reality.

I like to describe perception as a unique filter we all possess that creates our individual reality - how we see ourselves and others in the world. This filter is made up of the sum total of our unique life experiences from childhood into adulthood. Because we all have different experiences, we form different beliefs, which causes differences in our perception. We each perceive the world in our own unique way. You can picture this filter as your own personal mosaic where all of the pieces of your life experience come together and reflect how you see the world.

Perception is very powerful because it shapes our thoughts and attitudes and dictates our response in any situation. We all see something different even when looking at the same thing. Most disagreements are due to different perceptions. We may not be able to change certain situations or people, but we can choose how we view them. It's simply a matter of changing focus and perspective. We must look for what is right rather than what is wrong. How we view our circumstances determines what we get.

We have all heard the phrase "garbage in, garbage out." While intended to describe a concept in computer programming, it also can be used to describe what happens when we are giving our attention to the wrong things. Just as a computer can only do what it is programmed to do, we can only do what our minds have been programmed to do. To change our behavior we must change our internal programming. We speak and act from the programs running on the inside of us which are a result of what we have allowed into our mind through our eyes and ears.

When computer programs do not behave as intended by the program designer, the programmer performs a process called "debugging" which is a process of finding and fixing the defects in a computer program so that its functioning will result in the intended outcome. We must make a commitment to submit our minds to the debugging process. We must identify those internal programs that are in conflict with the Word of God and we must remove those programs and replace them with godly programs by renewing our minds.

Are You a Lunatic or a Moron?

Have you ever noticed anyone driving slower than you is a moron, and anyone driving faster than you is a lunatic? I remember the day I read these words many years ago. I couldn't stop laughing. I thought to myself surely someone must have planted a bug in my car! I can't count how many times over the years I made these claims and similar ones about other drivers.

I love this question because it illustrates our propensity to be "self" centered. I am not talking about self centered in the sense of selfishness, but rather being "self" centered when it comes to judging the world around us. We tend to judge the actions of others according to our own standard of behavior as we view our standard as the correct one.

One day as I was driving down the interstate another driver whizzed past me. At that moment it dawned on me the other driver probably thought I was a moron, while at the same time I was calling him a lunatic! Since I typically drive ten to fifteen miles per hour over the posted speed limit, anyone who whizzes past me at twenty to twenty-five miles per hour over the limit is a surely a lunatic. However, to that lunatic I am the moron who is going too slow. On other days I am the lunatic who rides up on the bumper of the moron who has the audacity to drive the posted speed limit!

In this scenario, the classification of lunatic or moron is based solely on my perception of my driving experience. In fact, my assessment has no basis in truth. Furthermore, my driving behavior is not correct. When I am driving 80 mph in a 70 mph zone, I am violating the posted speed limit, yet I get angry with those who are law abiding citizens and I expect them to get out of my way. I have no right to be angry with anyone since I have chosen to violate the law.

This simple illustration shows how our perception is our center from which we judge other people and the circumstances around us. Our perception is relative.

What Do You See?

In sports, referees are charged with making calls based on what they see. If you have watched any sporting events, you have noticed there are many instances when the referee makes a call based on what he saw at the time of the play, but when the play is reviewed on instant replay, the call was found to be incorrect. It confirms what he thought he saw did not actually happen. It is only by looking at the play from a different angle or point of view he can see what actually occurred causing the initial call to be reversed. In life we make "calls" based on what we see, or rather what we think we see. Unfortunately in life we don't have the advantage of instant replay to look at an occurrence frame by frame.

Awhile back I read the book *Quantum Faith* by Annette Capps. The book approaches the subject of faith from the perspective of quantum physics. In the book Capps states: *"You actually create your own reality. Your perception of life becomes your life."* [11] Wow! So if that is true, what do I need to do to change my life? I simply need to change my perception.

Perception is much more powerful than we realize. Perception shapes our thoughts and attitudes and also dictates our responses in situations. Most disagreements in life are simply due to perceptions. Stop for a moment and think of your most frequent disagreements with your significant other or someone else very close to you. Do you feel like a broken record? Do you feel like you are talking to a brick wall? Why do disagreements many times seem to go around in circles with no resolution? It is because each party is trying to get the other to see things from their perspective.

This became painfully obvious to me after my most recent relationship ended. Even after it ended, I still found myself arguing my case, but to no avail. One day I finally came to the realization there was nothing I could say or do that would cause my ex-boyfriend to view things any differently than he had during our time together or even to view things any differently now. Am I saying I was right and he was wrong? No. We each simply held a different view of how the relationship should be as well as what the relationship actually was to each of us. His complaints were as valid to him as mine were to me, even if each of our grievances may have been based on wrong perceptions.

In his book *I Once Was Blind But Now I Squint How Perspective Affects Our Behavior*, Kent Crockett says we don't see things alike because we wear different "sunglasses". Although each of us may be looking at the same exact thing, we see differently because we are all wearing a different pair of sunglasses.[12] For example, if Mary is wearing a pair of glasses with red lenses she can only see red. If John is wearing a pair of glasses with purple lenses he can only see purple and likewise if Susie's glasses have green lenses, then Susie can only see green. So what happens if I were to hold up a white piece of paper and ask Mary, John and Susie what each of them sees? Mary would see a red piece of paper, John would see a purple piece of paper and Susie would see a green piece of paper. Each of them would insist they are right, however, they would all be wrong. None of them will be able to see the paper as white until they remove the colored lenses.

Below is a drawing of a popular optical illusion. What do you see?

At first glance you will see either a young, beautiful woman or you might see an ugly, old woman. Which did you see? Perhaps you were able to see both. What allowed you to see a different image from the one you saw initially? It was changing your focus. For example, if you saw the young, beautiful woman at first glance, but then chose to focus in on her neck, you might have noticed the chin of an ugly old woman.

Any given situation in life is filled with varying images – we can choose to see the "ugly" in a situation or we can choose to see what is "beautiful" in a situation. Whether we see the ugliness or the beauty in a situation or within a person is simply a matter of refocusing. I am not suggesting we live in denial and escape to a fantasy world, but rather we carefully choose what we focus on. Any given day has both beautiful moments as well as ugly moments, and some days, well, let's face it, might be filled with mostly ugly ones. However, we simply need to train ourselves to refocus and look for the beauty in every circumstance. In your relationships choose to spend your time focusing on what is right, rather than what is wrong and you will see the quality of your relationships improve.

Some of you might be reading this and thinking – *Well that's easy for you to say. You have no idea what I have been through or what I am going through!* And my response to that would be - *You are absolutely right, I don't. Neither do you know what I have been through or what I go through on a daily basis.* I write this, not just to encourage you to look for and focus on the beauty around you, but as a reminder to myself to do the same.

We may not be able to change certain situations, but we can choose how we view those situations. How we view our circumstances and how we view others determines exactly what we get. It is true our perception determines our reality. Our perception of a person or situation may or may not be based in truth. In fact, I would venture to say in most cases our perception, although it is real to us, is not truth, but simply a point of view. Our perspective is not what we see, but the way we see it.

If we perceive life to be unfair, life is unfair. If we perceive we can never get ahead, we will never get ahead. If we perceive someone is rejecting us, our experience is one of rejection and we are rejected. If we perceive we are a victim and are constantly being victimized, we will always be a victim. On the other hand if we perceive life to be filled with endless possibilities it is. If we perceive we can rise above our circumstances we do. If we perceive we are loved, we are accepted. If we perceive we are a victor, we are victorious.

Set Your Mind & Keep It Set

If then you have been raised with Christ [to a new life, thus sharing His resurrection from the dead], aim at and seek the [rich, eternal treasures] that are above, where Christ is, seated at the right hand of God. [2] *And* ***set your minds and keep them set on what is above*** *(the higher things), not on the things that are on the earth.* [3] *For [as far as this world is concerned] you have died, and your [new, real] life is hidden with Christ in God.* **~ Colossians 3:1-3 AMP**

In Colossians, we are instructed to set our minds on "higher things"; to have a mindset focused on godly things. We must train ourselves in developing the habit of thinking God's thoughts. When our thoughts are contrary to God's Word, we must learn to exchange our thoughts for God's thoughts. We must take our thoughts captive and renew our minds with the Word of God. You must choose what you are going to set your mind on. When our mind is fixed on something, our mind will not change from day to day. Choose to set your mind on the Word of God and keep it set.

For those who are according to the flesh and are controlled by its unholy desires ***set their minds on*** *and pursue those things which gratify the flesh, but those who are according to the Spirit and are controlled by the desires of the Spirit* ***set their minds on*** *and seek those things which gratify the [Holy] Spirit.* **~ Romans 8:5 AMP**

As Christians, the spiritual realm should be more real to us than the natural realm. Does that mean we deny the facts or circumstances present in front of us? Absolutely not! It simply means we must recognize God is the highest authority and His will always prevails when we are operating in accordance with His Word even when circumstances in the natural seem to communicate the contrary. We cannot allow ourselves to be so caught up in our earthly circumstances it paralyzes us in our walk with God. We are in the world, but we are not of the world.[13] What we see now is only temporary.[14] We are dead to the world and alive in Him. Our new reality is in Christ.

Chapter 5

The Truth Will Set You Free

False Beliefs

So far we have learned many of our struggles as Christians are due to a battle between our soul and our born again spirit man. This inner conflict is due to a mind that has not been renewed. Hidden beliefs programmed in our subconscious prevent us from receiving God's best for us. These hidden beliefs consist of false beliefs which contribute to unbelief. Unbelief and wrong beliefs contribute to our struggles in life.

We possess many hidden inner beliefs that are in conflict with God's Word, and those beliefs prevent us from fully receiving the Word of God into our hearts and living the abundant life God has promised to us. We must identify and uproot these wrong beliefs to win the battle in our soul. These false beliefs must be addressed so we do not suffer the same fate as the Israelites. As we begin to renew our mind and identify our wrong ways of thinking and replace our thoughts with God's thoughts, it will become evident in our words and actions and we will see the manifestation of His promises.

To some degree, each one of us is living our life based on lies we believe. At first that seems like a hard pill to swallow, but unless you are 100% sanctified and transformed into the image of Christ, there are false beliefs lurking below the surface.

Can you relate to any of the following statements?

- No one loves me.
- I am all alone.
- God is mad at me.
- God doesn't love me.
- God cares for others more than me.
- I am unworthy.
- The best way to avoid more hurt and rejection is to isolate myself.
- My value is based on others' opinion of me.
- I need to take care of myself, because no one else will.
- No matter what I do it is never enough.

Although these statements may seem true to you, in reality each one of these statements is a false statement. Taking that a step further, these statements are actually lies. We believe lies about ourselves, God, others or a combination of all three. Too often we do not even realize many of our core beliefs are comprised of lies.

Chester and Betsey Kylstra of Restoring the Foundations ministry coined the term "ungodly beliefs" to describe the lies we believe. When I first heard that terminology it really hit home with me. It revealed the serious nature of the faulty beliefs I carried. If we acknowledge our wrong thoughts and beliefs as ungodly, it communicates to us the vital necessity of ridding ourselves of these beliefs.

So what exactly is an ungodly belief? According to the Kylstras, ungodly beliefs make up our belief system and consist of *"all beliefs, decisions, attitudes, agreements, judgments, expectations, vows and oaths that do not agree with God's Word, His nature or His character."*[1] To keep it simple, consider an ungodly belief any belief you possess that in any way contradicts God and His Word. Since He and His Word are absolute truth, anything in contradiction is a lie. We must shift from operating based out of ungodly beliefs into operating out of godly beliefs which are *"all beliefs, decisions, attitudes, agreements, judgments, expectations, vows and oaths that agree with God's Word, His nature and His character."*[2] To make the shift we must identify and uproot the lies we believe and replace them with the truth by renewing our minds with the Word of God. When we have adopted a godly belief we will begin to experience true transformation as evidenced by our character which is the product of a renewed mind. When a godly belief is properly rooted, it stands firm in the face of challenge.

Ungodly beliefs keep us from fulfilling God's will for our lives. They keep us stuck in the desert wandering around the same mountain over and over until we perish, just as the Israelites did. When we possess these beliefs, we hinder God's ability to manifest His promises in our lives. Our beliefs will always determine what we receive.

How False Beliefs Are Formed

The majority of our beliefs and belief systems are formed during the earliest years of our lives and are developed through our observations of the world around us. False beliefs are often birthed from our childhood experiences, in particular from hurts or traumas we experience. They may also be formed as part of the belief-expectation cycle (Chapter 4). We fall into a trap in which lies we believe appear to be true based on the "facts" of our experiences, yet are absolutely false when we judge them against God's Word. Every single belief we hold must be judged against the Word of God. If a belief is in contradiction with His Word then we must reject it and replace it with His truth. This is how we renew our minds. We must exchange the lies we believe for His thoughts which are eternal truths.

Facts vs. Truth

To exchange our thoughts for God's thoughts, we must be able to distinguish facts present in the natural realm from the eternal truth of God's Word. Although certain facts may exist in the natural, there is a higher level of truth than facts we see in nature. The fact may be you have a medical report diagnosing a disease, but the higher truth of God's Word says by the stripes of Jesus you are healed.[3] God's Word has already been settled in heaven and it will not return void when it is planted and cultivated properly. God cannot deny Himself. It is up to us to appropriate His Truth and bring His will into fruition here on earth.[4]

When a circumstance is contrary to a promise of God it is not truth. It may be a fact in the natural realm, but it is not truth. Consider your unpleasant circumstance merely as circumstantial evidence. The enemy is well versed in using circumstantial evidence to hurl accusations at us. His tactic is to get us to believe something that is not true or does not exist. He causes us to question God's Word and he wants to convince us God's Word is not true and God will not do what He said He would do. His tactic with Eve in the Garden of Eden was to twist God's instruction and get her to question what God had said. Eve chose to believe Satan's words instead of God's words and all of mankind suffered the consequences.

> *The serpent was the shrewdest of all the wild animals the LORD God had made. One day he asked the woman, "Did God really say you must not eat the fruit from any of the trees in the garden?" 2 "Of course we may eat fruit from the trees in the garden," the woman replied. 3 "It's only the fruit from the tree in the middle of the garden that we are not allowed to eat. God said, 'You must not eat it or even touch it; if you do, you will die.'" 4 "You won't die!" the serpent replied to the woman. 5 "God knows that your eyes will be opened as soon as you eat it, and you will be like God, knowing both good and evil." 6 The woman was convinced. She saw that the tree was beautiful and its fruit looked delicious, and she wanted the wisdom it would give her. So she took some of the fruit and ate it. Then she gave some to her husband, who was with her, and he ate it, too.* ~ **Genesis 3:1-6 NLT**

Choose to Agree with God

We have a choice to agree with what God says or agree with what the enemy says. Amos 3:3 says, *can two walk together, unless they are agreed?* To walk with God, we must get into agreement with Him and His Word. When we believe the lies of the enemy, we are choosing to believe what he says over what God says and we open up the door to receive in accordance with what we believe. We must break agreement with any lies and replace them with the truth of God's Word. Only then will we experience freedom and see the results of His Word working in our lives.

God has placed before us the same choice He placed before the Israelites and we get to choose what we believe.

> *15 "Now listen! Today I am giving you a choice between*
> *life and death, between prosperity and disaster. 16 For I*
> *command you this day to love the LORD your God and to*
> *keep his commands, decrees, and regulations by walking*
> *in his ways. If you do this, you will live and multiply, and*
> *the LORD your God will bless you and the land you are*
> *about to enter and occupy. 17 "But if your heart turns*
> *away and you refuse to listen, and if you are drawn away*
> *to serve and worship other gods, 18 then I warn you now*
> *that you will certainly be destroyed. You will not live a*
> *long, good life in the land you are crossing the Jordan to*
> *occupy. 19 "Today I have given you the choice between life*
> *and death, between blessings and curses. Now I call on*
> *heaven and earth to witness the choice you make. Oh,*
> *that you would choose life, so that you and your*
> *descendants might live! 20 You can make this choice by*
> *loving the LORD your God, obeying him, and committing*
> *yourself firmly to him. This is the key to your life. And if*
> *you love and obey the LORD, you will live long in the land*
> *the LORD swore to give your ancestors Abraham, Isaac,*
> *and Jacob."* ~ **Deuteronomy 15:15-20 NLT**

Effects of Ungodly Beliefs

In our relationships with others, the lies we believe cause us to have a distorted picture of reality and cause us to take everything personally. We tend to always magnify things and be on the defensive. Anger is often boiling under the surface and manifests itself in many destructive behaviors. Our behaviors based on our false beliefs strain all of our interpersonal relationships as we accuse and hurt others. If you are unable to find joy in your relationships and have a pattern of failed relationships, then ungodly beliefs surely play a part.

The lies we believe wreak havoc in our lives in so many different ways. First and foremost, they keep us from fulfilling our God given destiny and possessing all God has for us. Second, our false beliefs have a profound effect on our relationships with ourselves, God and others. We are unable to see ourselves as God sees us so we don't have an understanding of our worth and value as a child of God. Our faith is eroded as we are filled with guilt and condemnation believing God is mad at us and therefore He is not going to bless us. Additionally, the lies we believe affect our relationship with God because we have a distorted picture of Father God. God's blessings are hindered in our lives because of our unbelief.

Examples of Ungodly Beliefs

During my time of personal ministry, I was amazed at the lengthy list of ungodly beliefs revealed and those were only the tip of the iceberg! Identifying these false beliefs is a life-long process as God works with us and reveals them in various stages. The following is a list of some of my ungodly beliefs identified as part of my *Restoring the Foundations Ministry* sessions. Can you relate to any of these?

- I must have the answer or solution for everyone and everything.
- No matter what I do it is never enough.
- God loves others more than He loves me.

- I can't submit to God completely because He may make me do something I do not have the ability to do or He may make me do something I do not want to do.
- God will not speak clearly to me when I need Him to.
- I must be strong and in control to protect and defend myself.
- I don't belong, or fit in anywhere, I am always on the outside looking in.
- I am not worthy to receive anything good from God.
- No one will love me just because I am me.
- My value comes from what I do, not from who I am.
- I have messed up so badly I have missed God's best for me.
- I am out here alone and there is no one to care for me or rescue me.
- If I do anything for God the enemy will hit me hard, I must remain passive to be safe.
- I am not good enough or worthy enough to have a good a man.
- God will not allow me to receive anything easily. He will always make me struggle to receive good things from Him.

That's quite a list, isn't it? When examined in its entirety, my list clearly reflects a distorted picture of both Father God and who I am in Christ. These distortions wreaked havoc in all of my interpersonal relationships. Interestingly, as I began to share this list with people who knew me, many couldn't believe these things I had on my list. After all, to most people I seemed to have it all together and none of them would have imagined I was such a mess on the inside. In many ways my life looked ideal as I was very careful to only show people what I wanted them to see.

Since the time I uncovered these ungodly beliefs, I have continued to discover many other issues lurking below the surface. I will be honest and tell you I still struggle with several of the beliefs on my list. Some of them I was able to overcome rather quickly and others are still a work in progress. Thankfully now that I possess the knowledge and revelation I do, I am able to identify issues more quickly and deal with them by surrendering them to God rather than being stuck in a rut repeating the same actions over and over again.

A good friend of mine took part in a ministry similar to my *Restoring the Foundations* experience and she identified several ungodly beliefs controlling her life. She was gracious enough to share some from her list. Perhaps you can relate to some of her statements as you did to some of mine:

- I cause others pain.
- God is disappointed in me.
- People would be better off if I didn't exist.
- God can't use me because I waited too long.
- I need to take care of myself, because no one else will.
- My needs are selfish.
- When I receive a gift, I have to give it to others, because to enjoy it for myself is selfish.
- I need to be productive even in my rest.
- Others don't really love me; they just tolerate me.

Here are some other common ungodly beliefs. How many of these echo your inner thought life?

- The best way to avoid more hurt and rejection is to isolate myself.
- My feelings don't count. No one cares what I feel.
- When something is wrong it is always my fault.
- I am a bad person. If people knew the real me they would reject me.
- Even when I give and do my best it is never enough.
- I am unattractive. God shortchanged me.
- No matter what I do, I can't change.
- When someone offends me I must cut them off and punish them.
- Authority figures will just use and abuse me.
- My value is based on others' opinion of me.

- I am not able to give or receive love.
- I must do whatever is necessary to please others and keep the peace at all costs.
- Things never seem to go my way.

Sometimes ungodly beliefs aren't hidden. Sometimes they are right out there in the open continuously playing in our conscious mind. If you took an inventory of your thought life you would be astounded at the number of thoughts you have that are based on lies. How many of the lies that I believed can you relate to? How about those of my friend? When looking at each of these lists in their entirety it is easy to see how believing lies such as these can have a profound effect on our lives as the sum total create strongholds.

Strongholds

When several lies are working in tandem with each other they create a stronghold. The New Oxford American Dictionary defines a stronghold as *"a place that has been fortified so as to protect it against attack"* or *"a place where a particular cause or belief is strongly defended or upheld"*.[5] A stronghold is a fortress that has been built in the mind that is constructed of many thoughts. Negative thoughts build upon one another and lend support to one another. Imagine each thought as a corresponding brick in a wall. To cause the fortress to collapse requires strategic hits, taking out key sections of the wall. Just as a fortress would consist of many building blocks so does a stronghold. A stronghold rarely consists of one soul issue, rather it is a combination of issues that reinforce and protect each other. A stronghold is a mindset that consists of wrong ways of thinking and protects itself at all costs. Its root is formed by a lie buried deep within the soul.

> *3For though we walk (live) in the flesh, we are not carrying on our warfare according to the flesh and using mere human weapons. 4For the weapons of our warfare are not physical [weapons of flesh and blood], but they are mighty before God for the overthrow and destruction*

of strongholds, [5][Inasmuch as we] refute arguments and theories and reasonings and every proud and lofty thing that sets itself up against the [true] knowledge of God; and we lead every thought and purpose away captive into the obedience of Christ (the Messiah, the Anointed One),
~ 2 Corinthians 10:3-5 AMP

The Greek word for stronghold used in this passage is *oxýrōma* which literally means *"a heavily fortified containment."* A stronghold can be described as a fortress in the mind that protects itself against attack. Figuratively, *oxýrōma* speaks of a false argument in which a person seeks "shelter" to escape reality, or what we might refer to in some cases as a defense mechanism.[6]

A stronghold seeks to keep us blinded from the truth. When confronted, a stronghold does not allow us to see truth when it is presented. A stronghold dodges and makes excuses. It creates a false argument in our mind, convincing us what we believe is truth, when in fact what we believe is a lie. Many of us have strongholds operating in our lives yet we don't realize it because strongholds are self protective.

The Word of God is the most powerful weapon of our warfare in tearing down strongholds as well as preventing them from being established. Therefore we must use it daily!

How Strongholds Are Developed

Many strongholds are developed in childhood. We develop wrong ways of thinking and wrong beliefs based on what we see happening around us as well as through things that happen to us. An incident need not be traumatic to give place to a wrong mindset, nor does repetition need to take place to "lock" something in. One time traumatic events can become the root of a stronghold.

Often strongholds take root in infancy and early childhood and we aren't even aware of it. It isn't until we become teenagers or adults we start to notice we are somehow "different" from others and there is "something wrong with us". As adults often we are acting out of a set of beliefs, our world view, that was established in our childhood, many of which are in error. We have developed many wrong beliefs about ourselves, God and others. Strongholds may be formed as part of the Belief-Expectation Cycle (Chapter 4).

Identifying Strongholds

Since strongholds seek to protect themselves, it can be difficult to identify them. Once formed, a stronghold develops a pattern of behavior. Unfortunately often we are not aware strongholds are present even as they control our behavior each and every day. One way to identify a stronghold is to look for any habitual actions or responses you may understand to be wrong behaviors or wrong responses. Strongholds cause us to repeatedly engage in behaviors we know are wrong, or engage in destructive behavior patterns such as addictions or failed relationships.

Sometimes the hold is so strong we even find ways of justifying why we act the way we do. Defense mechanisms are a sure sign of strongholds in operation. It is easy to observe these defensive behaviors in others, but admitting to ourselves we have these behaviors can be very difficult. Defense mechanisms may include:

- Making excuses for poor behavior
- Blaming others
- Taking out frustration on others
- Refusing to face the truth
- Habitual lying
- Withdrawal or fantasy
- Avoidance
- Passive-aggressive behavior

It is also important to look for what are called "knee jerk" reactions – those reflex reactions that are triggered by someone or something. For example, if you are easily offended or often experience anger towards others, chances are there is at least one stronghold in operation, and possibly more than one. If certain situations make you uncomfortable and bring fear and anxiety or anger, the reaction is rooted in a stronghold of some sort.

How we react to what others say and do says more about us than it does them. It doesn't matter whether their actions or words are right or wrong. Regardless, we must seek to identify why their words and actions stir us in the negative manner in which they do. Our emotional reactions to others serve as warning lights on our personal dashboard. When we are feeling anger, jealousy, fear, rejection or any other emotion, these emotions are an indicator of a deep rooted issue lying beneath the surface. Our strong reactions to others are due to a soul battle within us. It has little to do with them.

Dangerous Persuasions

Awhile back I stumbled upon a TV show called *Dangerous Persuasions*. The series features true stories of individuals who have fallen prey to psychological manipulation. The episode I saw recounted the story of a woman by the name of Colleen Stan who was kidnapped in 1977 while hitchhiking. She was held captive by a couple, Cameron and Janice Hooker, for over seven years.

After eight months of being brutally tortured and kept in a locked box for twenty-three hours a day, Cameron forced Colleen to sign a contract agreeing to be his slave for life. At the time he led her to believe she was being watched by a large, powerful organization called "The Company" which would painfully torture her and kill her family if she tried to escape. As Cameron reinforced this threat day after day, Colleen's greatest fear became what harm "The Company" might do to her and her family. Once Cameron was confident Colleen would not try to escape under the threat of harm, he began to allow her to go outside and even jog around the neighborhood. Often the couple left her at home alone to watch their young children. Even with an open door, access to neighbors and a telephone, Colleen made no attempt to escape which she said later was due to her fear of "The Company."

One day after four years in captivity, the Hookers allowed Colleen to go home to visit her family. Before Cameron dropped her off for a weekend visit, he warned her "The Company" was nearby watching her and listening to her every word. When she arrived at the family home, she claimed Cameron was her fiancé, but he could not stay. Her sister sensed something was wrong, but Colleen would not provide any details of the past four years under fear of the threat of "The Company." Colleen's captor returned for her and she willingly returned back to his home with him where she continued to be tortured.

The abuse continued and Colleen was kept in the locked box each day for several more years, but eventually Colleen was allowed out of the house to work as a maid at a local hotel. Although each day she was left alone at work she never tried to escape because she believed "The Company" was watching. Finally in 1984, after seven years, Cameron's wife Janice hit a breaking point with Cameron, as his behavior was escalating with plans to acquire additional female slaves. He had already murdered one he had kidnapped prior to Colleen. Janice went to visit Colleen at work and told her Cameron was not part of a group called "The Company", no one was watching her, and she could have left at anytime. With this revelation of truth, Colleen went back to the house with Janice and the two of them packed up their stuff and left. After seven years, Colleen was finally free.

The next day as I was driving in my car I couldn't stop thinking about the horrific story I had watched the night before. This woman who spent over seven years in captivity could have escaped the first time she was left alone or any other moment she was alone in the months and years that followed. She had countless opportunities to take off and run and never look back, yet she remained in bondage to this man day after day because of her fear of "The Company." The only thing truly holding Colleen captive for over seven years was the lie she believed. As soon as Janice told her the truth and she accepted it, she immediately fled and returned home. Colleen was now a free woman because she had discovered the truth and embraced it.

Believing one lie caused her to live in fear which kept her in bondage for all those years.

As I was reflecting on this story, it struck me this is exactly what our enemy, Satan, does to us. He and his demons are constantly whispering lies into in our ears. He tells us a lie, we choose to believe it and then we are living in bondage as a result of believing the lie. How many of us are living our lives based on his lies we have accepted as truth? What lies do we believe that are causing us to live in fear, keeping us in bondage and keeping us from God's perfect will for our lives? Too often we are making decisions based in fear – fear of what might go wrong, fear of what others may think, fear of the unknown and even fear of God punishing us – the list is endless.

We are only able to break free when we hear the truth that exposes the lie and we choose to accept the truth that replaces the lie. Like Colleen, we too can be free in an instant when we discover the truth and accept it as fact. So how do we replace a lie with truth?

1. We must identify the lie we believe. To keep it simple, a lie (ungodly belief) is anything contrary to the Word of God.

    Lie: I must be strong and in control to protect and defend myself.

2. We must find a scripture telling us what God says about the situation. The Word of God is our truth.

    Scripture: The Lord is my Strength and my [impenetrable] Shield; my heart trusts in, relies on, and confidently leans on Him, and I am helped; therefore my heart greatly rejoices, and with my song will I praise Him. **~Psalm 28:7 AMP**

3. We must break agreement with the lie by renouncing the lie and speaking the truth (godly belief).

    Truth: God is my shield and protector. As I

submit to Him and trust Him, He provides protection for me.

4. We must meditate on Scripture to renew the mind. We must exchange our thoughts and ideas for God's thoughts and ideas so we can live our lives according to His truth.

   Keep meditating on the statement of truth and the supporting scripture until you have fully accepted the truth and no longer believe the lie. Do this for as long as it takes. It may take only a few days or it may take a few months, or possibly even longer. Pray and ask God if there is another lie present reinforcing the one from which you are seeking to break free. Keep pressing on and do not allow yourself to become discouraged.

5. As the lie attempts to present itself to you again, you must refuse to accept it.

   2 Corinthians 10:5 instructs us to take every thought captive to the obedience of Christ. Speak out loud you are refusing to accept the lie and you choose to receive the Truth of God's Word. Speak the statement of truth and meditate on the supporting scripture until the negative thought leaves.

We should not willingly or passively accept any thoughts or beliefs contrary to the word of God. 1 Peter 5:8 AMP says:

> *"8 Be well balanced (temperate, sober of mind), be vigilant and cautious at all times; for that enemy of yours, the devil, roams around like a lion roaring in fierce hunger], seeking someone to seize upon and devour."*

Which lies of the enemy keep playing in your head? *I'm not good enough. God is mad at me. God doesn't love me. I will never succeed. I will never achieve my dreams. I must be in control. I am unworthy.* How are those lies holding you captive? I challenge you to take some time to follow the steps above and renew your mind with what God has to say about the situation so your life will be transformed. Refuse to allow the enemy to seize your mind with his lies. Do not allow his "dangerous persuasions" to keep you from experiencing God's best for your life.

Chapter 6

Sowing & Reaping

Now that you have an understanding of how ungodly beliefs can contribute to negative patterns in your life, we will explore the effects of judgments and inner vows. These often give birth to the ungodly beliefs we possess.

During my journey of discovery and healing I learned quite a bit about judgments, specifically bitter root judgments and inner vows. Most of my knowledge on this subject comes from the teachings of John and Paula Sanford of *Elijah House Ministries.*

Bitter Root Judgments

According to *Elijah House School for Prayer Ministry,* bitter roots are results of our sinful reactions to hurts formed when we make critical and condemning judgments of people and we are unable to forgive or refuse to forgive a person. A bitter root is not formed because of what happened to us, but rather out of our reaction of what happened to us. A bitter root may be formed due to a real *or perceived* wound.[1] As we have already learned, many times our perception of a situation does not reflect reality. The person who wounded us may never have intended to do so; in fact there may not have been anything malicious about what was said or done, but for some reason we perceive we have been slighted or insulted. We cannot control what others say to us or do to us, but we can control how we respond. Whether a real or perceived offense takes place does not matter, we must reserve judgment and walk in forgiveness.

One of the most quoted Scripture passages about judging others is from Jesus' Sermon on the Mount in Matthew 7:1-2 AMP:

> [1] *Do not judge and criticize and condemn others, so that you may not be judged and criticized and condemned yourselves.* [2]*For just as you judge and criticize and condemn others, you will be judged and criticized and condemned, and in accordance with the measure you [use to] deal out to others, it will be dealt out again to you.*

The Message Bible says it this way:

> *"Don't pick on people, jump on their failures, criticize their faults— unless, of course, you want the same treatment. That critical spirit has a way of boomeranging. How many times have you judged the actions of someone else only to find yourself eventually doing the very same thing that you condemned someone else for?* ~ **Matthew 7:1-5 MSG**

Have you ever found yourself repeating a behavior you disliked in someone else? Perhaps you vowed you would never say or do what the person did. How many of us have said *"I will never be like my mother"* or *"I will never be like my father"*, only to one day realize we are exhibiting the same behaviors we despised in one of our parents. This is a very common occurrence. Some might say this is true because we are a product of our environment, that we merely repeat what we have observed because we didn't have a healthy example and that in part might be true, but what I have learned has shown me it runs much deeper.

> *Therefore you have no excuse or defense or justification, O man, whoever you are who judges and condemns another. For in posing as judge and passing sentence on another, you condemn yourself, because you who judge are habitually practicing the very same things [that you censure and denounce].* ~ **Romans 2:1 AMP**

I believe The Message Bible translation best sums up the effects of bitter root judgments as it says, like a boomerang, what you put out comes back to you. Jesus said *"in accordance with the measure you [use to] deal out to others, it will be dealt out again to you."* Judgment is tied to the law of sowing and reaping.

> [7]***...For whatever a man sows, that and that only is what he will reap.*** [8] *For he who sows to his own flesh (lower nature, sensuality) will from the flesh reap decay and ruin and destruction, but he who sows to the Spirit will from the Spirit reap eternal life.* [9] *And let us not lose heart and grow weary and faint in acting nobly and doing right, for in due time and at the appointed season we shall reap, if we do not loosen and relax our courage and faint.* **~ Galatians 6:7-9 AMP**

When it comes to bitter root judgments we reap what we sow. When we judge someone, often we repeat the very same behavior we judged or we continue to be wounded in the same way. We either become the perpetrator of the behavior we condemned or we continue to be victimized in the same way. What is interesting is when we make ourselves the victim, our irrational expectancies and behaviors trigger undesirable behaviors in others and because of the belief expectation cycle, others confirm our ungodly belief, reinforcing the judgment.

When there are bitter root judgments against parents, evidence of their existence is most often found in relationship to a spouse or significant other. Often these judgments lie dormant until they are triggered. If mom was critical, a son may form a judgment all women are critical. When he gets married he will either end up with someone who is critical or he will perceive his wife is being critical even when she is not. If a father abandons his family or is not around, a daughter may form the judgment men cannot be depended on, and she may vow to take care of herself and claim she doesn't need a man.

Although the most common source of bitter root judgments may be from parents, hurts from other people during our foundational years may also cause us to form these judgments. A grandparent, aunt, uncle, brother, sister, a teacher or a babysitter may have wounded us in some way having a profound impact on us. However, bitter root judgments can also form when we are adults. They can form at any age.

> [37]*Judge not [neither pronouncing judgment nor subjecting to censure], and you will not be judged; do not condemn and pronounce guilty, and you will not be condemned and pronounced guilty; acquit and forgive and release (give up resentment, let it drop), and you will be acquitted and forgiven and released.* [38] *Give, and [gifts] will be given to you; good measure, pressed down, shaken together, and running over, will they pour [ad]into [the pouch formed by] the bosom [of your robe and used as a bag].* ***For with the measure you deal out [with the measure you use when you confer benefits on others], it will be measured back to you.*** **~ Luke 6:37-38 AMP**

In Luke 6, Jesus says not only are you not to judge others, but you must forgive others so you can be forgiven and released. He reiterates you will receive in accordance with what you give out. Very often verse 38 is quoted concerning finances, and while it is true God will bless you financially as you sow finances, I think it is important to note His statements about receiving immediately follow his admonition not to judge others and to forgive them.

Out of Your Own Mouth

> [12] *He therefore said, A certain nobleman went into a distant country to obtain for himself a kingdom and then to return.* [13] *Calling ten of his [own] bond servants, he gave them ten minas [each equal to about one hundred days' wages or nearly twenty dollars] and said to them, Buy and sell with these while I go and then return.*

> *14 But his citizens detested him and sent an embassy after him to say, We do not want this man to become ruler over us. 15When he returned after having received the kingdom, he ordered these bond servants to whom he had given the money to be called to him, that he might know how much each one had made by buying and selling. 16 The first one came before him, and he said, Lord, your mina has made ten [additional] minas. 17 And he said to him, Well done, excellent bond servant! Because you have been faithful and trustworthy in a very little [thing], you shall have authority over ten cities. 18 The second one also came and said, Lord, your mina has made five more minas. 19And he said also to him, And you will take charge over five cities. 20Then another came and said, Lord, here is your mina, which I have kept laid up in a handkerchief. 21For I was [constantly] afraid of you, because you are a stern (hard, severe) man; you pick up what you did not lay down, and you reap what you did not sow. 22He said to the servant,* ***I will judge and condemn you out of your own mouth,*** *you wicked slave! You knew [did you] that I was a stern (hard, severe) man, picking up what I did not lay down, and reaping what I did not sow? 23Then why did you not put my money in a bank, so that on my return, I might have collected it with interest? 24 And he said to the bystanders, Take the mina away from him and give it to him who has the ten minas.* **~ Luke 19: 12-24 AMP**

This passage is often used in lessons of stewardship, but one day as I was reading it, verse 22 was illuminated, *"He said to the servant, I will judge and condemn you out of your own mouth, you wicked slave!"* This reminded me of Jesus words: *"For just as you judge and criticize and condemn others, you will be judged and criticized and condemned, and in accordance with the measure you [use to] deal out to others, it will be dealt out again to you."*

In Luke 19, the slave was judged and condemned in accordance with his own words spoken of his master. The servant judged the nobleman as harsh and hard and that is exactly what he reaped. When the other servants were rewarded, what little this man had was taken away from him and given to the servant who had the most. The other servants did not judge, criticize or condemn.

It might very well have been true the man was harsh and hard because we are told his citizens detested him, but it was not the place of the servant to judge. He should not have concerned himself with what the master was or was not doing. Rather than judging the master's actions, he should have concerned himself with faithfully fulfilling his responsibility to his master. The servants who fulfilled their responsibility without judgment were rewarded.

The Word of God is very clear we are not to judge others and if we do we will face consequences of our actions. Jesus instructs us to examine ourselves and not to judge the actions of others. We will be judged according to the measure we deal out. If we do not want to be judged and we want to be forgiven, then we must not judge and we must forgive others. We will reap what we sow. We must exercise caution when we become hurt or offended, not to allow the hurt or offense to reside in our heart as a bitter root judgment.

The operation of a bitter root judgment may not be obvious. Often they are buried deep within our subconscious. When we make judgments early in life they are usually forgotten so we do not realize we have judgment and unforgiveness in our heart. Sometimes we may even believe we have forgiven others and we have made peace with our past when we have not.

Reaping on Bitter Root Judgments

In the book *Life Transformed* by John & R. Loren Sanford, they share a story of a woman who was plagued by a pattern of rejection. Friends continually abandoned her and her husband left her although she served each of them and was very self sacrificing. Due to some events in her past, she had formed a bitter root judgment all men and friends would leave her. This judgment caused her to act in a manner that caused them to reject her. She confessed her judgment and prayed. Afterwards her husband came home and her friends returned.[2]

Another compelling story comes from the book *Restoring the Christian Family* also by John Sanford. In it he shares the story of a woman who came for ministry who had been married three times. Her first husband forced her to work while he stayed home and drank all day and when she came home he would accuse her of cheating on him. She divorced him and then met and married her second husband, who a few months into the marriage also forced her to go to work while he stayed at home and drank. When she came home from work he would accuse her of cheating on him. After she divorced her second husband she was determined not to repeat the pattern. She met a Christian man who was responsible, well established and had several assets and he was never a drinker. One month after they were married her husband began to stay home and drink and sent her out to work and when she came home he accused her of adultery. When she first met her third husband he was nothing like the prior two, so what happened? During a time of ministry it was revealed that when she was a child her drunken father had forced her to work on the farm. After she finished working each day and came into the house he would accuse her of all kinds of things including fornication. Each man to whom she was married was behaving in the same manner as her father.[3]

So how do you know if you have a bitter root judgment operating in your life? In each case, neither woman understood why the negative patterns were present. Both had good intentions, yet they were not reaping the relationships they desired. Many of the problems we encounter in our interpersonal relationships can be attributed to bitter root judgments having the boomerang effect in our lives. Recurring patterns in relationships are a sure indicator. It is important to realize you may not always consciously remember bitter root judgments that are present. Although the hurt may have long been forgotten by the conscious mind, you will see the judgment producing bad fruit in your life.

Forgiveness

As you can see freedom comes not just from identifying a judgment, but it comes when you forgive the person you judged. Although someone may have wounded us deeply, we still must forgive. The requirement to forgive others and the consequences of unforgiveness are very clear in Scripture:

> 14 *For if you forgive people their trespasses [their reckless and willful sins, leaving them, letting them go, and giving up resentment], your heavenly Father will also forgive you.* 15 *But if you do not forgive others their trespasses [their reckless and willful sins, leaving them, letting them go, and giving up resentment], neither will your Father forgive you your trespasses.* ~ **Matthew 6:14-15 AMP**

> 21 *Then Peter came up to Him and said, Lord, how many times may my brother sin against me and I forgive him and let it go? [As many as] up to seven times?* 22 *Jesus answered him, I tell you, not up to seven times, but seventy times seven!* 23 *Therefore the kingdom of heaven is like a human king who wished to settle accounts with his attendants.* 24 *When he began the accounting, one was brought to him who owed him 10,000 talents [probably about $10,000,000],* 25 *And because he could not pay, his master ordered him to be sold, with his wife and his children and everything that he possessed, and payment to be made.* 26 *So the attendant fell on his knees, begging him, Have patience with me and I will pay you everything.* 27 *And his master's heart was moved with compassion, and he released him and forgave him [cancelling] the debt.* 28 *But that same attendant, as he went out, found one of his fellow attendants who owed him a hundred denarii [about twenty dollars]; and he caught him by the throat and said, Pay what you owe!* 29 *So his fellow attendant fell down and begged him earnestly, Give me time, and I will pay you all!* 30 *But he was unwilling, and*

he went out and had him put in prison till he should pay
the debt. 31 *When his fellow attendants saw what had*
happened, they were greatly distressed, and they went
and told everything that had taken place to their master.
32 *Then his master called him and said to him, You*
contemptible and wicked attendant! I forgave and
cancelled all that [great] debt of yours because you
begged me to. 33 *And should you not have had pity and*
mercy on your fellow attendant, as I had pity and mercy
on you? 34 *And in wrath his master turned him over to the*
torturers (the jailers), till he should pay all that he owed.
35 *So also My heavenly Father will deal with every one of*
you if you do not freely forgive your brother from your
heart his offense. ~ **Matthew 18:21-35 AMP**

When we do not forgive others, our unforgiveness imprisons us as it causes inner turmoil and torment. Furthermore, it will cause us to have difficulty in our relationship with God and we will not be able to walk in the fullness of what He has prepared for us.

To forgive means to grant relief from payment, cancel a debt; pardon, excuse offense without a penalty; cease to feel resentment against an offender.[4] True forgiveness is giving up resentment and surrendering your right to be paid back. I heard someone say it is like tearing up an IOU towards another. The truth is the person who offended you may never be able to pay you back or fully right the wrong, but Jesus can do so as you surrender your pain to Him and choose to forgive the one who offended you.

Forgiveness is a choice. It is not a feeling. If you are waiting to forgive someone until you feel like it, chances are it may never happen. You must make a decision to forgive because God requires us to forgive others. Forgiveness is a key that unlocks the door to freedom in every area of your life. It delivers you out of the hands of the tormentors and into the arms of a loving God.

A question I always struggled with was, *how do we know if we have truly forgiven someone? How can we be sure our heart has been cleansed from all unforgiveness?* There were times I said I had forgiven someone, but over time I came to the realization I had not. *Elijah House School for Prayer Ministry* offers the following checklist to help you determine when unforgiveness is present:

- Do you have strong emotional reactions when you see the person who hurt you?
- Do you want to try to avoid the person?
- Do you replay the hurt over and over again in your mind?
- Do you rehearse long speeches you would like to deliver to the person who hurt you?
- Do you imagine ways of getting even and getting revenge?
- Can you sincerely bless the person?
- Do you rejoice when good things happen for the person who wounded you?[5]

If you answered yes to the first five questions or answered no to the last two questions, the process of forgiveness towards the offender is not complete. The nature of these questions demonstrate forgiveness in a process. True forgiveness may not happen in an instant. If we are honest, often we think the person who hurt us doesn't deserve good things to happen to them. When you have truly forgiven someone you will be able to rejoice for them when good things happen. I find when I start praying for God to bless the person, eventually I get to the point where I sincerely want God to bless the person. At first I may not feel like praying for them or blessing them, but over time my feelings catch up as I honor God by obeying His Word.

A major reason why we don't forgive is we mistakenly believe when we choose to forgive someone we are saying what the offender did was not wrong and the offender is not accountable. That simply isn't true. Furthermore, forgiveness does not mean we must deny our hurt and anger, nor does it mean we must forget the offense occurred. However, we can surrender our hurt and pain to God and allow Him to heal our broken heart.

Inner Vows

Have you ever said *"I will not" "I will never"* or *"I will always"*? If so, you have made an inner vow. When we judge the behavior of a parent we may say *"I will never be like mom"* or *"I will never be like dad."* Our judgment of her/his behavior has caused us to form a vow. Judgments support our inner vows causing us to become like our mother or father committing the same acts we despised in them. When we judge another person and vow never to do what they did, often we find ourselves guilty of doing the same thing we judged someone else for doing. Our vow works in reverse and we get the boomerang effect.

As previously discussed, judgments may take root as a result of being wounded and often when we make a judgment we may form a vow. It is important to remember, judgments and inner vows may be made as a result of a real or perceived wound. Some of the most common inner vows are made as a result of how we view the actions of our parents during our childhood, but can be formed at any age.

Inner vows are very powerful because they program our subconscious to respond according the vow. Even as the vow is long forgotten, it will continue to control our lives. An inner vow programs our heart and mind to respond in a certain way. These inner vows control us and affect the quality of our relationships.

Here are some examples of inner vows:

- I will never let anyone hurt me again.
- I will always be in control.
- I will never trust anyone.
- I will never be like mom/dad.

Inner vows similar to *"I will always be in control"* or *"I will never let anyone hurt me again"* may be based on a judgment people are not safe and cannot be trusted. These judgments and the resulting vows are very common when we are repeatedly wounded by others, whether the wounds are real or perceived.

In his book *Growing Pains: How to Overcome Life's Earliest Experiences to Become All God Wants You to Be,* John Sanford says, *"An inner vow is a determination set by the mind and heart into all the being, usually early in life. It is a key element in the "fortress" we build in our heart to protect us from pain."*[6] Sanford's definition shows us how inner vows can be responsible for forming and reinforcing a stronghold. An inner vow, like a stronghold, controls our thoughts and actions and it can keep us imprisoned causing us to repeat the same pattern of behavior over and over again.

At one time or another all of us have made inner vows. They can be difficult to identify because they are often hidden in the subconscious, particularly if the vow is made in childhood. Hidden vows exercise great power over us by controlling many of our thoughts and actions each and every day. Negative patterns of behavior are an indicator of inner vows at work and may be responsible for why the Word of God we hear and know is not producing the desired fruit in our lives. Just as with ungodly beliefs, identifying inner vows and breaking agreement with them is an important key in being transformed by the renewing of our minds. We must provide an environment in which the Word of God can be planted, take root, and produce a harvest as was discussed in Chapter 3.

Inner vows are not only very powerful in controlling our emotions and behaviors, but they can have a profound effect on our physical bodies. John Sanford shares a story of a woman who came to him and his wife for ministry after being unable to give birth to a male child. Each time she had conceived a boy, she would miscarry around the beginning of the second trimester. Her doctors could not find a physical cause for the miscarriages. As the Sanfords questioned her about her childhood, she recalled herself walking beside a river and throwing stones into it and saying *"I'll never carry a boy child. I'll never carry a boy child."* She made this vow in response to the brutal treatment she received from her brother. They had discovered the root of the problem. The woman was asked to pray and after she forgave her brother and broke the vow she had made, she was finally able to give birth to a healthy son.[7]

What modern science has revealed to us about the mind-body connection, Scripture revealed to us thousands of years ago. Our thoughts not only determine our actions, but our thoughts also affect our health. Your body responds to the way you think and feel. Negative thoughts cause negative emotions and those negative emotions place the body in a state of distress and various health problems begin to manifest. Negative emotions are toxic.

According to the latest estimates, experts claim 80% of all disease may actually be stress-related. Prolonged states of stress have actually been linked to the onset of auto-immune diseases. The word disease literally means "not at ease". When we are living in a constant state of turmoil, our mind and body are not at ease. A sick soul can eventually produce a sick body.

The Word of God is life to us – both spiritual and physical. As it nourishes our soul it gives strength and health to our physical body. 3 John 2 tells us our physical body is healthy to the degree our soul prospers and Proverbs 4:20-22 says:

> *20 My son, attend to my words; consent and submit to my sayings. 21 Let them not depart from your sight; keep them in the center of your heart. 22 For they are life to those who find them, healing and health to all their flesh.*

Our physical bodies respond to our inner turmoil. The key to emotional and physical well being is studying and meditating on the Word of God daily. When we submit ourselves to God and we begin to get our thoughts in agreement with God's Word, choosing to believe His Word and rely on Him and trust Him fully, we no longer will be living in a state of distress. Meditating on His Word brings healing and health to both body and soul.

Identifying Inner Vows

Some inner vows are easy to identify as you catch yourself speaking or thinking the words *"I will never"* or *"I will always"* and some inner vows are not so obvious. For example one of mine was *"I don't need anyone. I can take care of myself."* Indicators of inner vows are similar to those present with ungodly beliefs. This is because ungodly beliefs, judgments and inner vows all reinforce one another. Look for actions and words that trigger "knee-jerk" reactions including anxiety, fear and anger. Any time a defense mechanism is operating, there may be an underlying inner vow and judgment or ungodly belief.

An inner vow may be clearly connected to a bitter root judgment, or a connection may not be clear, but an associated judgment does not have to be present or be identified to break a vow. After we identify an inner vow we simply need to confess the vow, repent for making the vow, forgive those of whom we made judgments, and renounce the vow.

Power of Words

Ungodly beliefs, bitter root judgments and inner vows are all made up of words. The words may be spoken by us or spoken to us. Often the lies we are carrying around are due to words that were spoken to us as a child by a parent or some other authority figure. As a child you may have heard:

- You will never amount to anything.
- You're stupid.
- You can't do anything right.

These are examples of word curses. If these or similar words were spoken to you as a child, possibly now as an adult you are living below your potential, believing you can never measure up. Perhaps throughout your life you have continued to speak these words over yourself saying *'I am stupid. I can't do anything right. I will never amount to anything.'* reinforcing these beliefs each time. All of these statements are lies. Any other statement God would not say about you is a lie. Scripture tells us:

[10] For we are God's masterpiece. He has created us anew in Christ Jesus, so we can do the good things he planned for us long ago. ~ **Ephesians 2:10 NLT**

[10] For we are God's [own] handiwork (His workmanship), recreated in Christ Jesus, [born anew] that we may do those good works which God predestined (planned beforehand) for us [taking paths which He prepared ahead of time], that we should walk in them [living the good life which He prearranged and made ready for us to live]. ~ **Ephesians 2:10 AMP**

[11] For I know the thoughts and plans that I have for you, says the Lord, thoughts and plans for welfare and peace and not for evil, to give you hope in your final outcome. ~ **Jeremiah 29:11 AMP**

Words others speak over us only carry power in our lives if we allow them to do so. The words we speak about ourselves are the most important. We do not have the ability to control the words others speak to us, but we are in control of what we accept as true. We should not accept the words of others as true unless the words spoken are words God would speak over us.

More important than the words others speak over us are the words we speak about ourselves. We are always drawn in the direction of our most dominant thoughts and we become what we say we are. Furthermore, we will receive in accordance with the words we speak. Luke 6:45 tells us out of the abundance of the heart the mouth speaks.

Recall the story of the Israelites. Over and over again they spoke of dying in the wilderness. Eventually that is exactly what happened.

[28] Now tell them this: 'As surely as I live, declares the LORD, I will do to you the very things I heard you say. [29] You will all drop dead in this wilderness! ~ **Numbers 14:28-29 NLT**

The Israelites received according to their words. Their words were rooted in unbelief and they did not believe the promises God had made to them. It was never God's will for them to perish in the wilderness, but because of their unbelief, they suffered the consequences. Likewise we will receive in accordance with what we believe and what we speak. That is why it is so important to root out all of the lies, judgments and vows we have planted in our heart. We do not want to continue to reap a harvest on those seeds we have planted; we want to uproot them and plant the seed of God's Word in our heart and mind to reap in accordance with His promises.

If you recognize you accepted a word curse spoken over you or if you have spoken a word curse over yourself, you simply need to pray and confess the words spoken, repent for speaking the word, break agreement with the words by renouncing them and speak the truth of God's Word.

Think Before Your Speak

Ungodly beliefs, bitter root judgments and inner vows are all made up of words. We must consider the power of the words we are speaking on a continual basis. We have the power to speak words of life or death about ourselves. Ungodly beliefs, bitter root judgments and inner vows expressed only in our thoughts are powerful enough to wreak havoc in our lives, but those which are continually verbalized carry even greater power as the words are constantly being reinforced each time we speak them. Too often we are using our words to curse and not bless, speaking death rather than life. We must learn to say what God says.

> [21] *Death and life are in the power of the tongue, and they who indulge in it shall eat the fruit of it [for death or life].*
> **~ Proverbs 18:21 AMP**

> [63] *It is the Spirit who gives life; the flesh profits nothing. The words that I speak to you are spirit, and they are life.*
> **~ John 6:63 NKJV**

Whenever we speak God's words, we are speaking life. We must make a choice to say what God says about us. Furthermore when speaking to others, we should speak over them as God would speak over them. Words have creative power. Our words can be used to bless or they can be used to curse.

> *8 But the human tongue can be tamed by no man. It is a restless (undisciplined, irreconcilable) evil, full of deadly poison. 9 With it we bless the Lord and Father, and with it we curse men who were made in God's likeness! 10 Out of the same mouth come forth blessing and cursing. These things, my brethren, ought not to be so. 11 Does a fountain send forth [simultaneously] from the same opening fresh water and bitter? 12 Can a fig tree, my brethren, bear olives, or a grapevine figs? Neither can a salt spring furnish fresh water.* ~ **James 3:8-12 AMP**

In the book, *The Power of the Blessing,* author Kerry Kirkwood, says concerning James 3, *"The tongue may be named as the culprit, but in actuality, it is an unrenewed mind or heart that feeds the tongue it's content."*[8] It is critical we renew our minds with the Word of God as discussed in Chapter 3. Our thoughts and words go hand in hand. That is why it is so critical we uproot all of the lies, inner vows and judgments planted in our hearts and minds. What we meditate on and what we have planted in our heart will determine what we say.

In Philippians we are provided instruction regarding our thought life:

> *8 For the rest, brethren, whatever is true, whatever is worthy of reverence and is honorable and seemly, whatever is just, whatever is pure, whatever is lovely and lovable, whatever is kind and winsome and gracious, if there is any virtue and excellence, if there is anything worthy of praise, think on and weigh and take account of these things [fix your minds on them]. For the rest, brethren, whatever is true, whatever is worthy of*

reverence and is honorable and seemly, whatever is just, whatever is pure, whatever is lovely and lovable, whatever is kind and winsome and gracious, if there is any virtue and excellence, if there is anything worthy of praise, think on and weigh and take account of these things [fix your minds on them]. **~ Philippians 4:8 AMP**

When we get our heart and mind right, we will be able to speak and live right.

29Let no foul or polluting language, nor evil word nor unwholesome or worthless talk [ever] come out of your mouth, but only such [speech] as is good and beneficial to the spiritual progress of others, as is fitting to the need and the occasion, that it may be a blessing and give grace (God's favor) to those who hear it. 30And do not grieve the Holy Spirit of God [do not offend or vex or sadden Him], by Whom you were sealed (marked, branded as God's own, secured) for the day of redemption (of final deliverance through Christ from evil and the consequences of sin). 31Let all bitterness and indignation and wrath (passion, rage, bad temper) and resentment (anger, animosity) and quarreling (brawling, clamor, contention) and slander (evil-speaking, abusive or blasphemous language) be banished from you, with all malice (spite, ill will, or baseness of any kind) **~ Ephesians 4:29-31 AMP**

According to God's standard, it is never acceptable to speak any words other than those that bring life. We are even called to bless our enemies.

44 But I say to you, love your enemies, bless those who curse you, do good to those who hate you, and pray for those who spitefully use you and persecute you, 45 that you may be sons of your Father in heaven; for He makes His sun rise on the evil and on the good, and sends rain on the

> *just and on the unjust. [46]For if you love those who love you, what reward have you? Do not even the tax collectors do the same? [47]And if you greet your brethren only, what do you do more than others? Do not even the tax collectors do so? [48]Therefore you shall be perfect, just as your Father in heaven is perfect.* ~ **Matthew 5:44-48 NKJV**

In *The Power of the Blessing,* Kirkwood shares a story of a pastor who on a daily basis would pass by a neighborhood strip club and curse it. It seemed for all his efforts, the club actually seemed to flourish. He couldn't understand why it was flourishing because God was on his side, wasn't He? One day as he was on his way to curse the club the Lord spoke to him and asked him *"Why are you cursing the people that I have given my life for – the same life that I gave for you?"* From that question the pastor had revelation the club patrons were blinded to the truth:

> "Like someone learning a new language, the pastor began to bless the owner of the club and the people inside. At first it was awkward, but he felt the pleasure of the Lord while blessing them. He realized it was the goodness of the Lord that brings people to repentance. Within two weeks, the once-thriving club had shut their doors without any notice. Cursing causes darkness to thrive, and blessing turns things for righteousness sake. What the pastor learned is a lesson that many Christians never seem to grasp. Blessing is an attribute of God. This took the weight off his shoulders – the burden of having to punish his foes. A new strategy for spiritual warfare was opened to him."[9]

What a revelation! God does not want us using our words to curse others, nor does he want us using our words to curse ourselves. Jesus gave his life for you, for me and for every other person on the planet. For God so loved the world, he gave His only begotten son that whosoever believes in Him shall not perish, but have everlasting life.[10] It is not His will for anyone to perish, regardless of what they have done.

Determining Your Harvest

Our thoughts and words are seeds. When we accept a thought it becomes a belief and our thoughts are reflected in our words. Each time we speak words we are planting seeds. Based on the words you are speaking, what type of harvest are you planting? The law of sowing and reaping applies to our words. We cannot speak death and expect to reap life, we cannot speak cursing and expect blessing. Our words shape our future.

If the Word of God we know is not working for us, then chances are something is not right within us. Rather than getting angry with God and blaming him for what is wrong in our lives, we must take a serious self-inventory beginning with an examination of our thoughts and our words.

> 19 *God is not a man, that He should tell or act a lie, neither the son of man, that He should feel repentance or compunction [for what He has promised]. Has He said and shall He not do it? Or has He spoken and shall He not make it good?* ~ **Numbers 23:19 AMP**

> 3*What if some did not believe and were without faith? Does their lack of faith and their faithlessness nullify and make ineffective and void the faithfulness of God and His fidelity [to His Word]?* 4*By no means! Let God be found true though every human being is false and a liar, ...* **~ Romans 3:3-4 AMP**

> 10 *As the rain and the snow come down from heaven, and do not return to it without watering the earth and making it bud and flourish, so that it yields seed for the sower and bread for the eater,* 11***so is my word that goes out from my mouth: It will not return to me empty, but will accomplish what I desire and achieve***

> ***the purpose for which I sent it.*** **~ Isaiah 55:10-11 AMP**

If God said it, He will do it. Period. God is not a man that He should lie. His Word will not return void. It will always go forth and accomplish what He sent it to do. The unbelief of the Israelites did not nullify God's will. God said He would bring the Israelites into the Promised Land and He did. It was the unbelieving generation that shut themselves out. The only ones allowed to enter from the generation which left Egypt were Joshua and Caleb because they believed they were well able to take the land God had given them.

The Choice is Yours

In Numbers 22 we are presented with the story of Balaam and Balak. Balak, the king of Moab, was fearful of the large number of Israelites and their strength. He wanted Balaam to curse the Israelites so the Moabites would be assured victory over them. Imagine the surprise of Balak when Balaam spoke blessing over the Israelites three times! Balaam informed Balak he did not have the power to curse the Israelites because they were operating under the blessing of God.

> *And God said to Balaam, You shall not go with them; you shall not curse the people, for they are blessed.*
> **~ Numbers 22:12 AMP**

> *How can I curse those God has not cursed? Or how can I [violently] denounce those the Lord has not denounced?*
> **~ Numbers 23:8 AMP**

> *You see, I have received His command to bless Israel. He has blessed, and I cannot reverse or qualify it.*
> **~ Numbers 23:20 AMP**

Although Balaam stated the blessing of God, could not be reversed, Balaam motivated by greed and obtaining payment if he was able to bring a curse upon the Israelites, advised Balak to place a stumbling block in the path of the Israelites.

> *14 Nevertheless, I have a few things against you: you have some people there who are clinging to the teaching of Balaam, who taught Balak to set a trap and a stumbling block before the sons of Israel, [to entice them] to eat food that had been sacrificed to idols and to practice lewdness [giving themselves up to sexual vice].* ~ **Revelation 2:14 AMP**

Balaam knew while he did not possess the power to curse the Israelites, they had the power to bring calamity upon themselves through acts of disobedience to God.

> *Israel settled down and remained in Shittim, and the people began to play the harlot with the daughters of Moab, 2 Who invited the [Israelites] to the sacrifices of their gods, and [they] ate and bowed down to Moab's gods. 3 So Israel joined himself to [the god] Baal of Peor. And the anger of the Lord was kindled against Israel.* **~ Numbers 25: 1-3 AMP**

God's will was to bless Israel, but because of their disobedience they suffered the consequences. The choices of some of the Israelites kept them from God's best for them. However, in the next several verses in Numbers 25, God in his infinite mercy provided a plan of redemption for them. He has done the same for each of us so we can press on toward the territory He has prepared for us.

God was very clear in His instruction to the Israelites. He gave them a choice - a choice between life or death.

> *15 "Now listen! Today I am giving you a choice between life and death, between prosperity and disaster. 16 For I command you this day to love the LORD your God and to keep his commands, decrees, and regulations by walking in his ways. If you do this, you will live and multiply, and the LORD your God will bless you and the land you are about to enter and occupy. 17 "But if your heart turns away and you refuse to listen, and if you are drawn away*

to serve and worship other gods, [18] then I warn you now that you will certainly be destroyed. You will not live a long, good life in the land you are crossing the Jordan to occupy. [19] "Today I have given you the choice between life and death, between blessings and curses. Now I call on heaven and earth to witness the choice you make. Oh, that you would choose life, so that you and your descendants might live! [20] You can make this choice by loving the LORD your God, obeying him, and committing yourself firmly to him. This is the key to your life. And if you love and obey the LORD, you will live long in the land the LORD swore to give your ancestors Abraham, Isaac, and Jacob." ~ **Deuteronomy 15:15-20 NLT**

Satan and his demons are continually throwing stumbling blocks onto our path so we will cause our own demise. Since he has been stripped of his power, he knows the only means of gaining power over us is to get us to hinder the power of Word of God in our lives. If we are not careful, our wounds have a way of becoming stumbling blocks as we choose to walk in judgment, bitterness, and unforgiveness due to the pain we have suffered. Ungodly beliefs, inner vows and judgments are all stumbling blocks that lead to disobedience and keep us shut out of the abundant life God has promised us.

We negate the promises of God through our own free will by making choices that are not in agreement with His Word. He has provided us with instruction on how to walk in the fullness of His Word, but if we choose not to agree with Him and follow His leading, then we will not be able to access the power of God's Word. We have been given the same choice the Israelites were given. Prosperity or disaster. Life or death. The choice is ours. Whatever a man sows is what he will reap. He who sows to his own flesh will reap destruction, but he who sows to the Spirit will reap life.[11]

Chapter 7
Identity in Christ

If someone came up to you and asked '*who are you?*', how would you respond? Your first response probably would be your name. Your name identifies you legally, but it doesn't convey who you are. If the inquiry was posed a second time, you might respond with your occupation or your role as a wife or mother or husband or father. None of these answers reveal anything about your nature or your character - who you really are. Would it occur to you to answer with '*I am a child of the most High God, predestined to do good works according to His plan*' or '*I am the righteousness of God in Jesus Christ and I am more than a conqueror because of His power that lives in me*'? Probably not, but both of those responses are more on target than our typical responses, because they are based on God's eternal truth. Our problem is we do not view ourselves as God views us.

An Identity Crisis

Too many Christians are suffering from an identity crisis. Most have no idea who they are in Christ or otherwise have a very superficial understanding of who they are in Christ. *Merriam-Webster* defines an identity crisis as *"a feeling of unhappiness and confusion caused by not being sure about what type of person you really are or what the true purpose of your life is"*.[1] Too many Christians are walking around unfulfilled and confused about who they really are and why they are here.

We are created in God's own image and likeness.[2] It is our Creator who defines us and no one else. The labels others place on us are meaningless. It doesn't matter what any other person says about you, it only matters what God says about you. Anything said about you that does not agree with what God says about you is a lie.

Understanding your identity in Christ is essential to living the abundant life God has promised. In his book *Victory Over Darkness: Realizing the Power of Your Identity in Christ*, Neil T. Anderson says:

> "People cannot consistently behave in ways that are inconsistent with the way they perceive themselves. You don't change yourself by your perception. You change your perception of yourself by believing the truth. If you perceive yourself wrongly, you will live wrongly because of what you are believing is not true. If you think you are a no-good bum, you will probably live like a no-good bum. If, however, you see yourself as a child of God who is spiritually alive in Christ, you will begin to live accordingly. Next to the knowledge of God, knowledge of who you are is by far the most important truth you can possess. The major strategy of Satan is to distort the character of God and the truth of who we are. He can't change God and he can't do anything to change our identity and position in Christ. If, however, he can get us to believe a lie, we will live as though our identity in Christ isn't true."[3]

When we are unable to see ourselves as God sees us, we will suffer from a false identity. The enemy has deceived us into accepting his lies. His strategy is to fill our head with lies about who we are and to get us to believe God will not do what He said He will do. Each of us to some degree, possess faulty beliefs about ourselves, others and God.

Anderson goes on to say, *"Your understanding of who God is and who you are in relationship to Him is the critical foundation for your belief system and your behavior pattern as a Christian."*[4] Recall from chapter

4 our beliefs determine how we view ourselves, others and God. If we struggle to exhibit right behavior, we possess a faulty belief system. We must uncover each of the lies that contribute to our world view.

The Schemes of the Devil

The devil uses many schemes to prevent us from fulfilling the will of God for our lives, but the number one scheme of the devil is deception. Deception is an act of making someone believe something that is not true. Ungodly beliefs and inner vows are all are carefully constructed acts of deception. If Satan and his demons can't keep us from accepting Jesus Christ as our Lord and Savior, he will attempt to keep us blinded from the truth of God's Word by taking it out of context.

> *Now the serpent was more subtle and crafty than any living creature of the field which the Lord God had made. And he [Satan] said to the woman, Can it really be that God has said, You shall not eat from every tree of the garden? 2And the woman said to the serpent, We may eat the fruit from the trees of the garden, 3Except the fruit from the tree which is in the middle of the garden. God has said, You shall not eat of it, neither shall you touch it, lest you die. 4But the serpent said to the woman, You shall not surely die, 5For God knows that in the day you eat of it your eyes will be opened, and you will be like God, knowing the difference between good and evil and blessing and calamity.* ~ **Genesis 3:1-5 AMP**
>
> .....
>
> *13And the Lord God said to the woman, What is this you have done? And the woman said, The serpent beguiled (cheated, outwitted, and deceived) me, and I ate.* **~ Genesis 3:13 AMP**

Satan's schemes involve trickery and deceit. He is a master of deception, twisting and distorting God's words to suit his purposes. He did it with Eve in the Garden and he even did it with Jesus during his forty days in the desert! If Satan had the audacity to take Scripture out of context in an effort to tempt the Son of God, surely he will do the same with you.

> [3] *But I fear that somehow your pure and undivided devotion to Christ will be corrupted, just as Eve was deceived by the cunning ways of the serpent.* **~ 2 Corinthians 11:3 AMP**

In this verse, Paul was speaking about being led astray by false teaching, but his words make another important point. We must focus our attention on Jesus Christ and submit our minds completely to the Word of God, otherwise we run the risk of being deceived just as Eve was deceived. Since the devil has been stripped of his power, the only power he has is the power we give to him. The way we give him power is through believing his lies.

Ephesians 6:11 instructs us to put on the armor of God so we are able to stand up to the strategies and deceits of the devil. In the original text the strategies and deceits are referred to as "schemes" of the devil, the Greek word being *methodeía* representing *"a pre-set method used in organized evil-doing (well-crafted trickery)."*[5] The devil has been scheming against mankind since the Garden of Eden. The enemy knows each one of us is born with a God given destiny and he will stop at nothing to derail God's plan for our lives. From the time we are conceived, the devil is out to steal our destiny.

> [10] *The thief comes only in order to steal and kill and destroy. I came that they may have and enjoy life, and have it in abundance (to the full, till it overflows).* **~ John 10:10 AMP**

The Greek word for thief used in John 10:10 is *kléptēs,* which describes a thief who steals by stealth, rather than in the open with violence.[6] In executing his schemes, Satan operates like a stealth bomber flying under the radar, invading territories undetected. The main territory the devil is after is your mind. If he can get you to believe his lies, then he has defeated you.

> [8] *Be well balanced (temperate, sober of mind), be vigilant and cautious at all times; for that enemy of yours, the devil, roams around like a lion roaring in fierce hunger], seeking someone to seize upon and devour.*
> **~I Peter 5:8 AMP**

Our enemy is very subtle in his approach and he doesn't fight fair. From the time we are conceived, the enemy of our soul sets into motion a plan of destruction for our lives. A strategy of the devil is to paralyze us by getting us to believe lies about ourselves, others and God. Unfortunately, even as we grow spiritually, often we are still bound by invisible chains. When we are young, the attack on our mind is concealed as he begins planting destructive seeds from the moment we are born. He strikes before we become wise to his schemes. As children we do not have the cognitive abilities to process what is happening to us or around us, nor do we have full knowledge of the Word of God to defend ourselves. As children we are highly susceptible to being controlled by negative thoughts and behaviors. The hurts and traumas we experience as children have a profound impact on us and often keep us paralyzed as adults, stuck in negative patterns of behavior.

I do not believe the devil sits on our shoulder 24/7 whispering lies in our ears, rather I believe in many instances he sets the stage for us to create our own demise and we unknowingly and gradually work our way into his trap. I believe he plants seeds in our minds that we accept and then take on a life of their own. Once we accept a lie as true, his work in that area is accomplished as we will now behave in accordance with the lie we believe. As new lies are accepted and as each new lie reinforces the other, we become our own worst enemy as strongholds are formed.

When Satan cannot deceive us, he will do whatever it takes to destroy us and keep us from a relationship with God. If he can't keep us from accepting Jesus as our Lord and Savior, he will endeavor to keep us in bondage in our soul. He wants to keep us in a holding pattern so we will not fulfill God's will for our lives and he wants to rob us of God's promises.

Replaying the pain of our past experiences is one of the devil's greatest schemes. He wants to keep us chained to our past hurts and traumas causing us to wallow in our pit of pain, self-pity, rejection, shame and unworthiness topped off with bitterness and unforgiveness. We can choose to sit and lick our wounds, blaming others and blaming God for what has happened to us, but that will keep us stuck right where the enemy wants us. If our enemy is unable to deceive us, he will attempt to place stumbling blocks into our path through temptation and distraction.

The greatest weapon we possess to combat the schemes of our enemy, is the Word of God. Use your mighty Sword to defeat the lies the enemy attempts to plant in your mind. He is rendered powerless and ineffective when we know and apply the truth of God's Word. We must read it, speak it and choose to believe it. As we renew our mind with the Word, we will come to know who we are in Christ and the power and authority we possess and we will not fall prey to one of his most powerful schemes which involves getting us to adopt a false identity.

False Identity

A major key to walking in freedom is possessing an understanding of who we are in Christ and embracing our identity in Christ. Unfortunately strongholds operating in our lives constructed of the lies we believe mask our true identity and do not permit us to embrace who we are in Christ. In fact, the lies we believe actually cause us to form a false identity.

A false identity is a form of an ungodly belief. It is a statement about who "I am" as a person that is a lie. Any "I am" statement that does not agree with what God says about you is a false identity statement. The enemy wants us to take on a false identity. He makes us think:

- I am unworthy.
- I am unlovable.
- I am stupid.
- I am a bad person.

The enemy knows if we obtain the full revelation of who we are in Christ and the power we have in Him, we will be an unstoppable force. He wants us to believe we are weak and powerless, not strong and victorious and powerful in Christ. He wants us to see ourselves as unworthy, undeserving and guilty. Once we receive revelation of who we are in Christ and we embrace that truth, the devil knows we have appropriated our victory over him and he can no longer lie to us and keep us in bondage.

Strongholds & False Identity

Often strongholds will cause us to take on a false identity. Although there are many different strongholds that exist, I would like to explore one in particular to illustrate how a stronghold operates. It is the shame-fear-control stronghold.

I chose this stronghold for two reasons. First, it is one I discovered at the root of many of my issues when I participated in *Restoring the Foundations* ministry. Second, Chester & Betsey Kylstra of *Restoring the Foundations* discovered this stronghold operating in approximately 80% of the thousands of individuals they ministered to over several decades.[7] I believe the majority of people reading this book also have this stronghold operating in their lives to some degree and are completely unaware of its presence. Prior to learning about this stronghold I could see clear evidence of fear and control in my life, but I had no idea why I struggled with fear and control. I did not know shame was a root cause.

As I began studying the shame-fear-control stronghold, it was no surprise to me most of us struggle with this stronghold to a certain extent. You might be asking like I did, *why would shame be so prevalent?* Perhaps it is because it is the first blow delivered to man as a result of Satan's deception in the Garden of Eden.

> *25 Now the man and his wife were both naked, but* ***they felt no shame.*** *The serpent was the shrewdest of all the wild animals the LORD God had made. One day he asked the woman, "Did God really say you must not eat the fruit from any of the trees in the garden?" 2 "Of course we may eat fruit from the trees in the garden," the woman replied. 3 "It's only the fruit from the tree in the middle of the garden that we are not allowed to eat. God said, 'You must not eat it or even touch it; if you do, you will die.'" 4 "You won't die!" the serpent replied to the woman. 5 "God knows that your eyes will be opened as soon as you eat it, and you will be like God, knowing both good and evil." 6 The woman was convinced. She saw that the tree was beautiful and its fruit looked delicious, and she wanted the wisdom it would give her. So she took some of the fruit and ate it. Then she gave some to her husband, who was with her, and he ate it, too. 7 At that moment their eyes were opened, and* ***they suddenly felt shame*** *at their nakedness. So they sewed fig leaves together to cover themselves. 8 When the cool evening breezes were blowing, the man and his wife heard the LORD God walking about in the garden. So they hid from the LORD God among the trees. 9 Then the LORD God called to the man, "Where are you?" 10 He replied, "I heard you walking in the garden, so I hid. I was afraid because I was naked.". 11 "Who told you that you were naked?" the LORD God asked. "Have you eaten from the tree whose fruit I commanded you not to eat?" 12 The man replied, "It was the woman you gave me who gave me the fruit, and I ate it." 13 Then the LORD God asked the woman, "What have you done?" "The serpent deceived me," she replied. "That's why I ate it."* **~ Genesis 2:25, 3:1-13 NLT**

This event demonstrates how the shame-fear-control stronghold works.

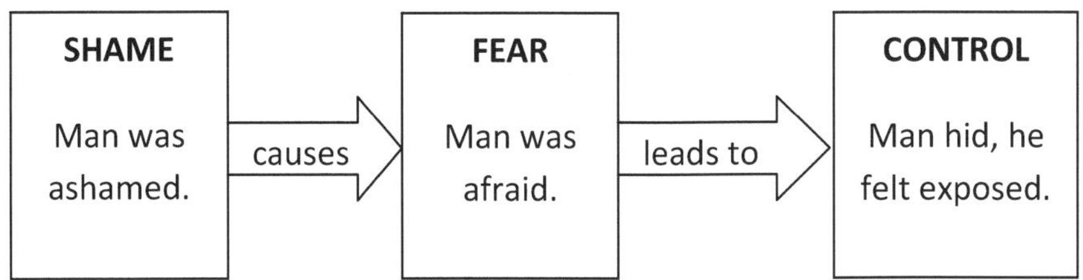

When we are rooted in shame, we become afraid of being exposed and of others seeing our flaws, so we seek to control situations and those around us to protect ourselves. Shame lies to us about who we are. Fear holds us back from God's best. Control creates a boomerang effect because as we try to protect ourselves from hurt and pain, we experience more hurt and pain.

> [25]*Now the man and his wife were both naked, but* ***they felt no shame.*** **~ Genesis 2:25 NLT**

Adam and Eve felt no shame in the presence of God, although they were exposed. There was nothing separating them from God.

> [4] *"You won't die!" the serpent replied to the woman.* [5] *"God knows that your eyes will be opened as soon as you eat it, and you will be like God, knowing both good and evil."*
> [6] *The woman was convinced.* **~ Genesis 3:4-6 NLT**

Shame was brought about by believing a lie. Shame causes us to believe lies about ourselves.

> [7]*At that moment their eyes were opened, and* ***they suddenly felt shame*** *at their nakedness. So they sewed fig leaves together to cover themselves.* **~ Genesis 3:7 NLT**

At that moment, they felt ashamed and exposed, so they sought to cover their shame.

> [8]*When the cool evening breezes were blowing, the man and his wife heard the* LORD *God walking about in the garden. So they hid from the* LORD *God among the*

trees. ~ **Genesis 3:8 NLT**

Their shame caused them to hide from God because they did not want to be exposed. As such, it separated them from God.

> *He replied, "I heard you walking in the garden, so I hid (CONTROL). I was afraid (FEAR) because I was naked (SHAME)."* ~ **Genesis 3:10 NLT**

Man retreated and hid from God because of his shame.

> *[11]"Have you eaten from the tree whose fruit I commanded you not to eat?" [12] The man replied, "It was the woman you gave me who gave me the fruit, and I ate it." [13] Then the LORD God asked the woman, "What have you done?" "The serpent deceived me," she replied. "That's why I ate it."* ~ **Genesis 3:11-13 NLT**

Through Eve accepting a lie of the enemy, shame was brought to mankind. Notice shame brought about blame. Adam blamed Eve and Eve blamed Satan. This is what shame does – it points the finger at others. It is our attempt to shift responsibility to those around us as we try to convince ourselves we are not responsible for our own behavior. When we shift blame and refuse to accept responsibility for our actions, we are not able to walk in all that God has prepared for us.

Satan knew the power of shame to destroy. He knew shame would cause Adam and Eve to be separated from God. Just as Satan has been shamed, he seeks to bring shame to others. The first defeat he suffered was when he decided he was going to exalt himself above God he was cast down out of heaven. His second and ultimate defeat was when Jesus died on the cross for our sins.

> *[13] You were dead because of your sins and because your sinful nature was not yet cut away. Then God made you alive with Christ, for he forgave all our sins. [14] He canceled the record of the charges against us and took it*

> *away by nailing it to the cross.* [15] *In this way, he disarmed the spiritual rulers and authorities. He shamed them publicly by his victory over them on the cross.* **~ Colossians 2:13-15 NLT**

Shame has been with us since the beginning so is it any wonder shame would afflict each of us at some point and to some degree? Shame is such a potent weapon and our enemy knows the power of shame. Shame robs us of our true identity in Christ and masks our true identity in Him. In fact it causes us to take on a false identity. Shame says *"I am bad. I am a mistake."* It robs us of our destiny because we are so consumed by our fear and our desire to control the people and situations in our lives. Shame operates under the fear of being exposed. Shame protects itself. It does not want to be exposed therefore it seeks to defend itself at all costs. When it is on the verge of being exposed it will deny its own existence.

Shame is based on lies and it lies to us about who we are. *Restoring the Foundations Ministry* teaches that shame says *"I am bad. I am different from everyone else."* Fear says *"I am afraid if anybody finds out how bad I am they will not accept me, approve of me, or love me."* Control says *"I have to control my environment and everyone in it so no one discovers my defect."* Control may even lead to rebellion which causes one to resist, get angry, hate, scheme, and strategize to regain control if they feel they are being controlled. The person in rebellion will revolt against any authority or person in a position of power or a perceived position of power. Also if threatened, he or she will withdraw to avoid being controlled and/or exposed.[8]

Shame vs. Guilt

The Psychoanalysis Dictionary defines shame as *"a sense of anxiety about being, excluded, unloved and not accepted."*[9] I like Brené Brown's definition in her book *I Thought It Was Just Me (but it isn't): Making the Journey from 'What Will People Think?' to 'I Am Enough'.* In it she says, *"Shame is the intensely painful feeling or experience of believing we are flawed and therefore unworthy of acceptance or belonging."*[10]

I have read several different books and articles and they all seem to agree shame says *"I am bad"* and guilt says *"I did something bad."* Those steeped in shame believe *"I am a mistake"*, but guilty people believe *"I made a mistake."* Guilt can actually serve us in a positive manner in changing future behavior, if we don't let it consume us, but shame only serves to keep us imprisoned. The Holy Spirit will convict us, when we are doing wrong, but He will not condemn us, shame us or cause us to wallow in guilt.

Spiritually speaking, shame is a SHAM! A sham is a "trick that deludes",[11] and that is exactly what shame does. It deludes you into thinking you are bad, unworthy, unlovable, etc., when in fact those thoughts are delusions – false beliefs and opinions! These types of thoughts are in direct contradiction to your true identity – your identity in Christ. To delude means to impose a misleading belief upon someone, deceive, or fool.[12] Satan has deluded the body of Christ with his tricks. Since the beginning he has presented lies as truth.

> [44] *You are of your father, the devil, and it is your will to practice the lusts and gratify the desires [which are characteristic] of your father. He was a murderer from the beginning and does not stand in the truth, because there is no truth in him. When he speaks a falsehood, he speaks what is natural to him, for he is a liar [himself] and the father of lies and of all that is false.* ~ **John 8:44 AMP**

Shame is at the root of many lies we believe and it continually feeds and reinforces those lies. The shame-fear-control stronghold is broken by dismantling all of the lies that have formed the stronghold.

Take a few moments to answer the following questions:

- Do you have difficulty believing what God says about you?

- Are you unable to overcome your past although you want a better future?
- Do you have difficulty receiving love?
- Do you constantly make poor decisions and live in regret?
- Do you engage in destructive habits? (i.e. substance abuse, self-mutilation, eating disorders, dysfunctional relationships)
- Do you repeatedly settle for less than you deserve?

If you answered yes to several of these questions, then you are likely living your life based on a false identity masked by shame. Here are some additional questions to consider:

- Do you seek to be beyond criticism and fault? Do you "know it all"? (perfectionism)
- Do you feel you can never do anything good enough? Do you feel like you are stuck on the hamster wheel and can't get off? Does the feeling of satisfaction seem to constantly elude you? (performance oriented)
- Do you constantly find fault with others? Are you always putting others down? Do you constantly make comparisons? Are you overly competitive?
- Do you always expect defeat? Do you constantly blame your circumstances or blame others? (victim mentality)
- Are you always trying to avoid conflict? Do you make decisions based on what others will think? (people pleaser)
- Are you constantly apologizing to others when there is nothing to apologize for? Do you feel everything is your fault? Do you constantly feel you are to blame? Do you feel like a burden?[13,14]

If you answered yes to several of these questions as well, that is a further indicator a root of shame exists.

Identity Statements

Until we fully embrace our identity in Christ, each of us are suffering from some form of false identity because of lies we believe about ourselves. The following is a list of several lies I believed about myself:

- I am unworthy.
- I am rejected.
- I am ashamed.
- I am fearful.
- I am guilty.
- I am unlovable.
- I am inadequate.
- I am inferior.
- I am controlling.
- I am trapped.
- I am sick.

Each of these statements is an identity statement. Although I knew what the Bible said about my identity in Christ, I certainly hadn't believed it. Each of these "I am" statements illustrated my actions were being controlled by a false identity.

When I began sharing my list with others, many people were quite surprised that I viewed myself in this way. What I portrayed on the outside certainly didn't match what was on the inside. Most people saw me as highly motivated and self-confident and full of courage. My outward actions were simply masking what I was really feeling on the inside. In many ways my inner turmoil and dysfunction served me well for most of my life as I climbed the ladder of success constructing a lengthy list of accolades and accomplishments along the way. Others may have looked at me in envy, but on the inside I was empty and unfulfilled in spite of all of the worldly success I had achieved. As I was going through the motions every day, I didn't realize it, but underneath it all I was seeking validation and constantly striving to prove my worth and value through my accomplishments. I was driven and ambitious for all of the wrong reasons.

The lies we believe whether they are ungodly beliefs, inner vows or false identity statements, will push us to extremes in our behavior. A false identity may cause one to be either hyper-driven as I was, or it may cause one to be stuck at the other end of the spectrum wallowing in untapped potential or constant failure. We either "live up to" the lies or we endeavor to deny their existence by creating a façade.

Overcoming False Identity

We overcome a false identity using the same method as we do to overcome any ungodly beliefs. First, we must identify the lie that we believe about our identity. Second, we must find a scripture that reveals the truth to us about who we are in Christ. Third, we must break agreement with the lie and begin speaking the truth of God's Word. Fourth, we must continue to meditate on the truth of God's Word until we fully embrace His truth about our identity and we no longer believe the lies. Moving forward, we must refuse to accept the lies the enemy will bring into our mind and we must make God the final authority on who we are. We must choose to identify with God's Word so the enemy cannot mask our true identity.

God's Word says the exact opposite of all of those things I believed about myself. According to God's Word:

- I am worthy.
- I am accepted.
- I am honorable and valuable.
- I am calm and peaceful.
- I am forgiven.
- I am loved.
- I am created in His image and likeness.
- I am valuable.
- I am healed and whole.
- I am secure.
- I am free in Christ.

These identity statements reflect the truth about who I am whether I believe it or not; they are a reflection of what God says about me *and you too*!

Knowing Your True Identity

The only way to know and embrace your identity in Christ is to renew your mind with what God says about you. The Word of God is our mirror that reflects our identity in Christ. It is important to look into that mirror daily so we will see what God sees.

On the following pages, you will find several identity statements and the supporting scriptures that reflect your identity in Christ. Meditate on these scriptures and speak these truths over yourself until you believe them in your heart.

- **I am a child of God.**
  But to all who believed him and accepted him, he gave the right to become children of God.
  ~ John 1:12 NLT

- **I have right standing with God because of Jesus sacrifice on the cross.**
  Therefore, since we have been made right in God's sight by faith, we have peace with God because of what Jesus Christ our Lord has done for us.
  ~ Romans 5:1 NLT

- **I am joined to the Lord as one spirit.**
  But the person who is joined to the Lord is one spirit with him.
  ~ 1 Corinthians 6:17 NLT

- **I am a part of Christ's body.**
  All of you together are Christ's body, and each of you is a part of it.
  ~ 1 Corinthians 12:27 NLT

- **I am complete in Christ.**
  So you also are complete through your union with Christ, who is the head over every ruler and authority.
  ~ Colossians 2:10 NLT

- **I am a part of God's family, adopted by Him. He takes great pleasure in me.**
  God decided in advance to adopt us into his own family by bringing us to himself through Jesus Christ. This is what he wanted to do, and it gave him great pleasure.
  ~ Ephesians 1:5 NLT

- **God has forgiven my sins, rescued me from darkness and made me His heir.**
  He has enabled you to share in the inheritance that belongs to his people, who live in the light. For he has rescued us from the kingdom of darkness and transferred us into the Kingdom of his dear Son, who purchased our freedom and forgave our sins.
  ~ Colossians 1:12-14 NLT

- **I belong to Jesus therefore I am free from the power of sin and I am no longer condemned.**
  So now there is no condemnation for those who belong to Christ Jesus. And because you belong to him, the power of the life-giving Spirit has freed you from the power of sin that leads to death.
  ~ Romans 8:1-2 NLT

- **The Holy Spirit lives in me guaranteeing me God's promises for me.**
  It is God who enables us, along with you, to stand firm for Christ. He has commissioned us, and he has identified us as his own by placing the Holy Spirit in our hearts as the first installment that guarantees everything he has promised us.
  ~ 2 Corinthians 1:21-21 NLT

- **Each day God continues to do a good work in me.**
  And I am certain that God, who began the good work within you, will continue his work until it is finally finished on the day when Christ Jesus returns.
  ~ Philippians 1:6 NLT

- **I can do anything because I draw my strength from Christ.**
  For I can do everything through Christ, who gives me strength.
  ~ Philippians 4:13 NLT

- **I am a child of God. I no longer practice sin.**
  We know that God's children do not make a practice of sinning, for God's Son holds them securely, and the evil one cannot touch them.
  ~ 1 John 5:18 NLT

- **God chose me and appointed me to bear good fruit. He will give me all that I ask according to His Word.**
  You didn't choose me. I chose you. I appointed you to go and produce lasting fruit, so that the Father will give you whatever you ask for, using my name.
  ~ John 15:16 NLT

- **My body is the temple of the Holy Spirit. His power lives in me.**
  Don't you realize that all of you together are the temple of God and that the Spirit of God lives in you?
  ~ 1 Corinthians 3:16 NLT

- **I am a new person in Christ. My past no longer defines me or has power over me.**
  This means that anyone who belongs to Christ has become a new person. The old life is gone; a new life has begun!
  ~ 2 Corinthians 5:17 NLT

- **I am God's masterpiece. He has good things planned for me.**
  For we are God's masterpiece. He has created us anew in Christ Jesus, so we can do the good things he planned for us long ago.
  ~ Ephesians 2:10 NLT

- **God loves me and I am without fault in His eyes.**
  Even before he made the world, God loved us and chose us in Christ to be holy and without fault in his eyes.
  ~ Ephesians 1:4 NLT

- **I am not fearful or timid. I have a spirit of power, love and self discipline.**
  For God has not given us a spirit of fear and timidity, but of power, love, and self-discipline.
  ~ 2 Timothy 1:7 NLT

- **I have the mind of Christ, therefore I am able to understand His Word.**
  For, "Who can know the LORD's thoughts? Who knows enough to teach him?" But we understand these things, for we have the mind of Christ.
  ~ 1 Corinthians 2:16 NLT

- **I have victory in this world because of the power of the Holy Spirit that lives in me.**
  But you belong to God, my dear children. You have already won a victory over those people, because the Spirit who lives in you is greater than the spirit who lives in the world.
  ~ 1 John 4:4 NLT

- **I am more than a conqueror through Christ.**
  No, despite all these things, overwhelming victory is ours through Christ, who loved us.
  ~ Romans 8:37 NLT

- **I am victorious through Jesus Christ.**
  But thanks be to God, Who gives us the victory [making us conquerors] through our Lord Jesus Christ.
  ~ I Corinthians 15:57 AMP

- **I have a rich and satisfying life through Jesus Christ.**
  The thief's purpose is to steal and kill and destroy. My purpose is to give them a rich and satisfying life.
  ~ John 10:10 NLT

- **I am alive in Christ and seated in heavenly places with Him.**
  For he raised us from the dead along with Christ and seated us with him in the heavenly realms because we are united with Christ Jesus.
  ~ Ephesians 2:6 NLT

- **I have been made right with God through Christ.**
  For God made Christ, who never sinned, to be the offering for our sin, so that we could be made right with God through Christ.
  ~ 2 Corinthians 5:21 NLT

- **I have been chosen by God to show others the goodness of God.**
  But you are not like that, for you are a chosen people. You are royal priests, a holy nation, God's very own possession. As a result, you can show others the goodness of God, for he called you out of the darkness into his wonderful light.
  ~ 1 Peter 2:9 NLT

- **As Jesus is so am I. I am part of His body.**
  ...as He is, so are we in this world.
  ~ I John 4:17 NKJV

- **I share God's nature and I am able to live a godly life.**
  By his divine power, God has given us everything we need for living a godly life. We have received all of this by coming to know him, the one who called us to himself by means of his marvelous glory and excellence. And because of his glory and excellence, he has given us great and precious promises. These are the promises that enable you to share his divine nature and escape the world's corruption caused by human desires.
  ~ 2 Peter 1:3-4 NLT

- **I have right standing with God.**
  Who dares accuse us whom God has chosen for his own? No one—for God himself has given us right standing with himself. Who then will condemn us? No one—for Christ Jesus died for us and was raised to life for us, and he is sitting in the place of honor at God's right hand, pleading for us.
  ~ Romans 8:33-34 NLT

- **I am loved by God.**
  No, despite all these things, overwhelming victory is ours through Christ, who loved us. And I am convinced that nothing can ever separate us from God's love. Neither death nor life, neither angels nor demons neither our fears for today nor our worries about tomorrow—not even the powers of hell can separate us from God's love. No power in the sky above or in the earth below—indeed, nothing in all creation will ever be able to separate us from the love of God that is revealed in Christ Jesus our Lord. **~ Romans 8:37-39 NLT**

Conclusion

A Divine Appointment

[3] He left Judea and returned to Galilee. [4] It was necessary for Him to go through Samaria. [5] And in doing so, He arrived at a Samaritan town called Sychar, near the tract of land that Jacob gave to his son Joseph. [6] And Jacob's well was there. So Jesus, tired as He was from His journey, sat down [to rest] by the well. It was then about the sixth hour (about noon). [7] Presently, when a woman of Samaria came along to draw water, Jesus said to her, Give Me a drink— [8] For His disciples had gone off into the town to buy food— [9] The Samaritan woman said to Him, How is it that You, being a Jew, ask me, a Samaritan [and a] woman, for a drink?—For the Jews have nothing to do with the Samaritans— [10] Jesus answered her, If you had only known and had recognized God's gift and Who this is that is saying to you, Give Me a drink, you would have asked Him [instead] and He would have given you living water. [11] She said to Him, Sir, You have nothing to draw with [no drawing bucket] and the well is deep; how then can You provide living water? [Where do You get Your living water?] [12] Are You greater than and superior to our ancestor Jacob, who gave us this well and who used to drink from it himself, and his sons and his cattle also? [13] Jesus answered her, All who drink of this water will be thirsty again. [14] But whoever takes a drink of the water

that I will give him shall never, no never, be thirsty any
more. But the water that I will give him shall become a
spring of water welling up (flowing, bubbling)
[continually] within him unto (into, for) eternal life.
15 The woman said to Him, Sir, give me this water, so that
I may never get thirsty nor have to come [continually all
the way] here to draw. 16 At this, Jesus said to her, Go, call
your husband and come back here. 17 The woman
answered, I have no husband. Jesus said to her, You have
spoken truly in saying, I have no husband. 18 For you have
had five husbands, and the man you are now living with is
not your husband. In this you have spoken truly. 19 The
woman said to Him, Sir, I see and understand that You
are a prophet..........25 The woman said to Him, I know that
Messiah is coming, He Who is called the Christ (the
Anointed One); and when He arrives, He will tell us
everything we need to know and make it clear to us.
26 Jesus said to her, I Who now speak with you am He.
27 Just then His disciples came and they wondered (were
surprised, astonished) to find Him talking with a woman
[a married woman]. However, not one of them asked Him,
What are You inquiring about? or What do You want? or,
Why do You speak with her? 28 Then the woman left her
water jar and went away to the town. And she began
telling the people, 29 Come, see a Man Who has told me
everything that I ever did! Can this be [is not this] the
Christ? [Must not this be the Messiah, the Anointed One?]
30 So the people left the town and set out to go to
Him...........39 Now numerous Samaritans from that town
believed in and trusted in Him because of what the
woman said when she declared and testified, He told me
everything that I ever did. 40 So when the Samaritans
arrived, they asked Him to remain with them, and He did
stay there two days. 41 Then many more believed
in and adhered to and relied on Him because of His
personal message [what He Himself said]. 42 And they told

> *the woman, Now we no longer believe (trust, have faith) just because of what you said; for we have heard Him ourselves [personally], and we know that He truly is the Savior of the world, the Christ.* ~ **John 4:3-19, 25-30, 39-42 AMP**

At the time of this divine appointment between Jesus and the woman at the well, Jews did not associate with Samaritans. In fact, although the most direct route to travel from Judea to Galilee, was a direct path through Samaria, Jews took a longer route around Samaria when traveling north. In usual fashion, Jesus acted in direct contrast to socially acceptable standards of His day. Several roads led to Galilee, but we are told it was *necessary* for him to go through Samaria. It was necessary, because He had a divine appointment with a Samaritan woman.

Around noon, upon arriving at the well in Sychar, Jesus sat down. He sat waiting for the woman who was about to arrive and draw water in accordance with her usual routine, which actually was quite unusual. It was customary for women to make the journey to draw water from the well early in the morning to avoid the heat of the day. Apparently the scorching heat was no match for the burn of the ridicule and scorn she faced from others each day because of her history and because she was living in sin.

When she arrived at the well, she didn't expect anyone to be there, especially a Jewish man! I imagine as she approached the well she was already planning a quick getaway, when Jesus suddenly asked her to give Him a drink. She was astonished a man, in particular a Jewish man would speak to her and extend a request to her. Of course Jesus didn't need the woman to give Him a drink. He asked her for a drink to open up a dialogue with her. Jesus wanted to give her the gift of His living water to wash away her guilt, condemnation and shame that had kept her isolated for so long.

The woman had heard about the Messiah and she was eagerly waiting for Him to come. Now here He is in Samaria, talking to her!

After Jesus reveals to her He is indeed the Messiah, she gets so excited she does not bother to draw water and leaves her water jar behind to return to her village. She returns proclaiming she has had an encounter with the Messiah. In that moment she forgot the shame of her past. She was no longer hiding in the shadows. The woman was now making a spectacle of herself as she went through her town testifying about her encounter with Jesus and proclaiming the Good News. On account of her testimony, many more Samaritans believed in Jesus and accepted Him. It is His desire to do the same with your life.

One detail that must not be overlooked in this encounter is Jesus met the woman *where she was at.* Throughout the New Testament we see that Jesus went out of His way for social outcasts and He spent most of His time with individuals the religious leaders of His day considered unworthy. In the same way Jesus met the woman at the well and the man at the pool of Bethesda, He wants to meet you where you are at also. It doesn't matter what you have or haven't done. No matter what your past or your present, He is waiting to welcome you with open arms. In His presence there is no judgment, no condemnation, only love and acceptance. It is the desire of His heart that you receive all He has provided for you.

I believe reading this book was a divine appointment for you which will set up a series of divine appointments with the Holy Spirit. He wants to show you your blind spots and reveal to you the lies and strongholds keeping you from God's best. Jesus wants to meet with you and make you whole. He desires for you to be free from shame, fear, unworthiness, rejection or whatever else may be keeping you in bondage. He longs for you to experience the superabundant life He died to give you.

Final Thoughts

> [3] *... How long will you be slack to go in and possess the land which the Lord, the God of your fathers, has given you?* ~ **Joshua 18:3 AMP**

This question was posed to several of the tribes of Israel after the Promised Land had been given to them. The Hebrew word for slack is *raphah* which means to sink or relax.[1] In Joshua 18, the battle-weary tribes had become complacent. The journey to the Promised Land had taken a lifetime. Although they made tremendous progress up to this point, they were still short of their final destination. They began to settle where they were at and were not actively pursuing their inheritance. Joshua knew if they did not move forward to claim their inheritance, their enemies would have time to regroup and strengthen and they ran the risk of losing ground they had fought so hard to gain.

The Voice Translation of Joshua 18:3 says, *"How much more time do you intend to waste before going to claim the land the Eternal God of your ancestors is giving to you"?* **I pray that you do not waste any more time settling for anything less than God's best for you.** This is not a time to relax where you are. Whether or not you receive God's promises for a life that is superabundant in quantity and superior in quality, is up to you. God has given you the title deed to a good land - your very own Promised Land, but you must drive out all of the inhabitants that cause you to stumble and you must get up and take possession of it. You must drive out bitterness. You must drive out unforgiveness. You must drive out all judgments. You must drive out all inner vows. You must drive out all lies. The good news is you do not have to do it alone. The Holy Spirit will meet you where you are at and lead you and guide you along the way. He is gentle and will only take you where you are ready to go. All you need to do is give Him permission to do a work in your heart and allow Him full access into the deepest parts of your soul. It is only when you are willing to give Him "all access" that you will be able to unlock the power of God's Word and walk in the fullness of his promises.

---

[18] And all of us, as with unveiled face, [because we] continued to behold [in the Word of God] as in a mirror the glory of the Lord, are constantly being transfigured into His very own image in ever increasing splendor and from one degree of glory to another; [for this comes] from the Lord [Who is] the Spirit. **~ 2 Corinthians 3:18 AMP**

Download the companion workbook at:
www.diamondshapers.com/allaccessworkbook

View the schedule and sign up for the companion online course for *All Access: Unlocking the Power of God's Word* at
http://www.diamondshapers.com/classes/

Notes

Introduction

1. http://biblehub.com/greek/4053.htm
2. http://en.wikipedia.org/wiki/Blind_spot_(vehicle)

Chapter 1

1. Romans 5:1
2. http://biblehub.com/greek/2137.htm
3. http://biblehub.com/greek/5590.htm
4. *John G. Lake: The Complete Collection of His Life Teachings.* Compiled by Roberts Liardon. (New Kensington, PA: Whitaker House, 1999)
5. Exodus 14:10-12
6. Colossians 1:3
7. Numbers 13:32
8. John 5:19
9. "Soul Battles" CD, Betsey Kylstra, Restoring the Foundations http://stores.rtfresources.org/soul-battles/

Chapter 2

1. http://biblehub.com/greek/770.htm
2. http://biblehub.com/greek/5185.htm
3. http://biblehub.com/greek/3584.htm
4. http://biblehub.com/greek/5560.htm
5. http://biblehub.com/greek/3553.htm
6. http://biblehub.com/greek/769.htm
7. http://biblehub.com/greek/2309.htm
8. http://biblehub.com/greek/4043.htm
9. http://biblehub.com/greek/3708.htm
10. http://biblehub.com/greek/1096.htm
11. http://biblehub.com/greek/5199.htm
12. Genesis 3:9
13. http://biblehub.com/greek/964.htm

14. http://biblehub.com/greek/4002.htm

Chapter 3

1. Dr. Bill Winston, *Transform Your Thinking, Transform Your Life,* (Tulsa, OK: Harrison House, 2008)
2. http://biblehub.com/greek/4964.htm
3. New Oxford American Dictionary. Oxford University Press, 2010.
4. 2 Corinthians 5:20
5. http://biblehub.com/greek/3339.htm
6. W.E. Vine, *Vine's Concise Dictionary of the Bible (Nashville, TN:* Thomas Nelson, 2005)
7. http://biblehub.com/greek/342.htm
8. W.E. Vine, *Vine's Concise Dictionary of the Bible (Nashville, TN:* Thomas Nelson, 2005)
9. I John 4:17
10. Isaiah 53:4-5
11. John 10:10
12. Mark 3:25
13. http://biblehub.com/hebrew/5315.htm
14. I Peter 1:23
15. http://biblehub.com/greek/2588.htm
16. http://biblehub.com/greek/1366.htm
17. Ephesians 6:17
18. http://biblehub.com/hebrew/1897.htm
19. Psalm 37:4
20. http://biblehub.com/hebrew/3820.htm
21. http://biblehub.com/greek/4561.htm

Chapter 4

1. http://www.thefreedictionary.com/mindset
2. New Oxford American Dictionary. Oxford University Press, 2010.
3. http://www.kmle.com/search.php?Search=mindset

4. New Oxford American Dictionary. Oxford University Press, 2010.
5. http://www.businessdictionary.com/definition/cognitive-belief-system.html
6. Chester & Betsey Kylstra, *Restoring the Foundations: An Integrated Approach to Healing Ministry, 2nd edition,* (Hendersonville, NC: Restoring the Foundations Publications, 2001)
7. Brian Klemmer, *If How-To's Were Enough We Would All Be Skinny, Rich & Happy,* (Tulsa, OK: Insight Publishing Group, 2005)
8. Ibid.
9. Ibid.
10. http://www.businessdictionary.com/definition/perception.html
11. Annette Capps, *Quantum Faith* ®, (England, AR: Capps Publishing, 2003)
12. Kent Crockett, *I Once Was Blind But Now I Squint How Perspective Affects Our Behavior*, (Chattanooga, TN: AMG Publishers, 2004)
13. John 15:19
14. 2 Corinthians 4:18

Chapter 5

1. Chester & Betsey Kylstra, *Restoring the Foundations: An Integrated Approach to Healing Ministry, 2nd edition,* (Hendersonville, NC: Restoring the Foundations Publications, 2001)
2. Ibid.
3. Isaiah 53:5
4. Matthew 6:10
5. New Oxford American Dictionary. Oxford University Press, 2010.
6. http://biblehub.com/greek/3794.htm

Chapter 6

1. *Elijah House School for Prayer Ministry: Basic I* (Elijah House, Inc., 2009)
2. John Loren Sanford & R. Loren Sanford, *Life Transformed,* (Lake Mary, FL: Charisma House, 2009)
3. John Loren Sanford & Paula Sanford, *Restoring the Christian Family,* (Lake Mary, FL: Charisma House, 2009)
4. New Oxford American Dictionary. Oxford University Press, 2010.
5. *Elijah House School for Prayer Ministry: Basic I* (Elijah House, Inc., 2009)
6. John Loren Sanford & Paula Sanford, *Growing Pains: How to Overcome Life's Earliest Experiences to Become All God Wants You to Be,* (Lake Mary, FL: Charisma House, 2008)
7. Ibid.
8. Kerry Kirkwood, *The Power of the Blessing,* (Shippensburg, PA: Destiny Image Publishers, 2010)
9. Ibid.
10. John 3:16
11. Galatians 6:9

Chapter 7

1. http://www.merriam-webster.com/dictionary/identity%20crisis
2. Genesis 1:27
3. Neil T. Anderson, *Victory Over Darkness: Realizing the Power of Your Identity in Christ,* (Ventura, CA: Regal Books, 1990)
4. Ibid.
5. http://biblehub.com/greek/3180.htm
6. http://biblehub.com/greek/2812.htm
7. Chester & Betsey Kylstra, *Restoring the Foundations: An Integrated Approach to Healing Ministry, 2nd edition,* (Hendersonville, NC: Restoring the Foundations Publications, 2001)

8. http://restoringyourlife.org/resources/belief-strongholds.html
9. http://drdivaphd.wordpress.com/2013/02/10/stop-dancing-with-shame/
10. Brené Brown, PhD, *I Thought It Was Just Me (but it isn't): Making the Journey from 'What Will People Think?' to 'I Am Enough* , (New York, NY: Penguin Group (USA) Inc., 2007)
11. http://www.merriam-webster.com/dictionary/sham
12. http://www.oxforddictionaries.com/us/definition/american_english/delude
13. "Shame-Fear-Control Stronghold " CD, Chester & Betsey Kylstra, Restoring the Foundations http://stores.rtfresources.org/shame-fear-control-stronghold/
14. Chester & Betsey Kylstra, *Restoring the Foundations: An Integrated Approach to Healing Ministry, 2nd edition,* (Hendersonville, NC: Restoring the Foundations Publications, 2001)

Conclusion

1. http://biblehub.com/hebrew/7503.htm

About the Author

Stacie L. Buck is the President & Founder of Diamond Shapers International, LLC in Stuart, FL. She is a public speaker, author and life coach. Diamond Shapers International was birthed out of her desire and passion to help others achieve their goals and dreams and fulfill their God given destiny.

After a highly successful career in the healthcare industry Stacie was ready for a new challenge and decided to expand her horizons and take her passion for teaching and employ it on a larger scale to empower individuals to achieve their dreams and goals by overcoming obstacles to success.

Stacie is a gifted speaker and teacher who now uses her own journey of healing and self discovery as a teaching tool for others and she shares insights she has learned from several years of personal study. Stacie's speaking and teaching style is down to earth and she is known for her transparency.

To learn more about Stacie and her speaking, writing and personal coaching services, visit her on the web at www.diamondshapers.com

Follow Stacie on Facebook:
https://www.facebook.com/diamondstacie

Follow Stacie on Twitter: @DiamondStacie

Email Stacie at: info@diamondshapers.com

Other Books by the Author

Transformed: Scriptures to Renew Your Mind
A 30 Day Devotional

In this 30 day devotional, through Scripture, author Stacie L. Buck shares:

- The importance of renewing mind and how to renew the mind
- Results of a renewed mind
- How to take thoughts captive
- How to overcome unbelief to appropriate God's promises
- And much, much more!

To order go to http://www.diamondshapers.com/product-category/products/

Need a Speaker for your small group or next event?

Stacie shows you how to transform your life by transforming your mind.

Stacie will lead you in how to:

- Renew your mind and change the way you think about God, yourself and others.
- Recognize negative patterns in your life and understand how they reveal your inner beliefs.
- Identify hindrances that are keeping you from God's best for you.
- Clear your path of all the obstacles holding you back from the victorious and abundant life you have been missing out on.
- Embrace your true identity in Christ.
- Win the "battles" raging in your soul and overcome shame, fear, rejection and more—once and for all!

What audiences have to say:

"I have to say that your presentation had to be one of the very best as far as maintaining everyone's interest, your ability to deliver in an effortless way and interweaving your personal experiences brilliantly. Not only were you clearly knowledgeable about your subject matter, you shared personal experiences with such style, grace and conviction that it touched my heart. I've since been able to use the concepts you shared in both my personal and professional life with true benefits realized." **~Sue R.**

"Not only did I enjoy your style of teaching, but you opened yourself up and shared your own struggles for the benefit of others. The more I

apply your techniques to my life, the more free I become from all that has held me back for years. Thank you so much for being open to what God wanted you to do, as I believe this is your true calling!" **~Danielle L.**

"Stacie has tremendous knowledge and revelation in the area of transforming the mind. She is articulate and well-spoken and uses real life examples to help audience members identify and overcome mindsets that are hindering them from having the lives they desire." **~Sue L.**

"Stacie is very inspirational and knowledgeable, and speaks with a comfortable, personable style. She relates to her audience by sharing her own personal experiences and bringing hope to hearts that feel discouraged and hopeless. She is gifted in helping people to shed light onto their path and see the things that are holding them back. Stacie walks them through their metamorphic process, ultimately leading them to wholeness and beauty within, preparing and guiding them to achieve their divine destiny." **~Deborah B.**

"Thank you for a wonderful and lively presentation! I appreciate the revelations you made—a difficult illness and your internal struggle with personal demons. Exposing yourself in front of a large group of people, well, I see it as an act of bravery." **~Craig B.**

"I always make it a point to attend Stacie's sessions, even when the program has several other options. Her energetic and thought-provoking presentations always provide me with a smile from the insights. It is clear when attending that she has given her heart and soul to presentation preparation in concept, content and delivery. Stacie's genuine presentations will cause you to reflect on your beliefs and be inspired by new concepts." **~ Perry E.**

Visit http://www.diamondshapers.com/speaking to fill out the speaking request form to schedule Stacie to speak at your next event.

Contact the Author

Stacie L. Buck

President & Founder

Diamond Shapers International, LLC

850 NW Federal Highway, #427

Stuart, FL 34994

(772) 287-8849

Email: info@diamondshapers.com

www.diamondshapers.com

Diamond Shapers

INTERNATIONAL, LLC

Transforming Minds, Transforming Lives

Our Mission

To transform the world by transforming minds and transforming lives.

Our Vision

To create a world in which those in the body of Christ are operating in their full potential both personally and professionally having maximum impact on the world.

Our Strategy

To provide education and resources that empower believers to renew their minds, receive God's promises and operate according to His Word.

www.diamondshapers.com

Diamond Shapers

INTERNATIONAL, LLC

Transforming Minds, Transforming Lives

About Diamond Shapers International, LLC

Diamond Shapers International, LLC was founded by Stacie L. Buck. Diamond Shapers International was birthed out of her desire and passion to help others achieve their goals and dreams and fulfill their God given destiny.

Since Stacie was a little girl she has had a passion for teaching and it was a long standing dream of hers to become a teacher. Her path to teaching has certainly been one that is non-traditional. She graduated Magna Cum Laude with a Bachelor of Science Degree from Health Information Management and spent twenty-two years working in the healthcare industry. During her career in health information management she served in many roles, but regardless of her job title her passion still remained – teaching others which fueled her desire to begin her own consulting business. For over a dozen years Stacie provided education to those within her organization as well as to outside organizations. She is a nationally known speaker and author for her healthcare specialty and she taught several courses at the local state college.

In addition to her love for teaching, Stacie enjoys serving others and mentoring others. During her healthcare career she served in numerous volunteer positions and leadership roles and received numerous service awards, including the Mentor Award from the American Health Information Management Association. Her peers describe her as a leader who inspires others and elevates the performance of those around her. Stacie is also known for taking complex subject matter and making it simple for her students.

After a highly successful career in the healthcare industry Stacie was ready for a new challenge and decided to expand her horizons and take her passion for teaching and employ it on a larger scale to empower individuals to achieve their dreams and goals by overcoming obstacles to success.

She now uses her own journey of healing and self discovery as a teaching tool for helping others and she shares insights she has learned from several years of personal study. Stacie's speaking and teaching style is down to earth and she is known for her transparency.

www.diamondshapers.com

Recommended Reading

Biblical Healing & Deliverance: A Guide to Experiencing Freedom From Sins of the Past, Destructive Beliefs, Emotional and Spiritual Pain, Curses and Oppression, Chester & Betsey Kylstra

I Once Was Blind But Now I Squint – How Perspective Affects Our Behavior, Kent Crockett

Released from Shame: Moving Beyond the Pain of the Past, Sandra D. Wilson

I Thought It Was Just Me (but it isn't): Making the Journey from 'What Will People Think?' to 'I Am Enough', Brené Brown, PhD

Victory Over Darkness: Realizing the Power of Your Identity in Christ, Neil T. Anderson

Renewing the Mind, Casey Treat

Transform Your Thinking, Transform Your Life, Dr. Bill Winston

Battlefield of the Mind, Joyce Meyer

Attachments: Why You Love, Feel and Act the Way You Do, Dr. Tim Clinton

Life Transformed, John Sanford & R. Loren Sanford

Growing Pains: How to Overcome Life's Earliest Experiences to Become All God Wants You to Be, John Loren Sanford & Paula Sanford

Restoring the Christian Family, John Loren Sanford & Paula Sanford

Letting Go of Your Past, John Loren Sanford

God's Power to Change, John Loren Sanford

If How-To's Were Enough We Would All Be Skinny, Rich & Happy, Brian Klemmer

Made in the USA
San Bernardino, CA
20 May 2014